The Savage

NEIL GRANT

THE SAVAGE TRADE

*

KESTREL BOOKS

KESTREL BOOKS
Published by Penguin Books Ltd
Harmondsworth, Middlesex, England

Copyright © 1980 by Neil Grant

All rights reserved. No part of this publication may be reproduced, stored in a retrieval system, or transmitted in any form or by any means, electronic, mechanical, photocopying, recording, or otherwise, without the prior permission of the Copyright owner.

First published 1980

ISBN 0 7226 5489 8

Set, printed and bound in Great Britain by
Fakenham Press Limited, Fakenham, Norfolk

Contents

1. 'That Miserable Company' 7
2. 'Afric's Golden Joys' 13
3. Kingdoms and Villages 26
4. The Tyrant Sugar 35
5. Kings and Caboceers 42
6. 'An End to Happiness' 57
7. Mean Coasts and Rotting Castles 67
8. Floating Coffins 78
9. The Merchants 103
10. The End of the Trade 116

Slavery in History 131
Illustrations and Acknowledgements 138
Index 142

Prince Henry of Portugal. His sailors were the first Europeans who raided African villages to capture slaves.

1

'THAT MISERABLE COMPANY'

First to sail far from Europe's sheltering shores into the unknown Sea of Darkness, as the Arabs called the Atlantic Ocean, were the Portuguese. Their caravels coasted Morocco's shore down to Cape Bojador. But there they stopped. For many years, Bojador marked the limit. Beyond it, said the Portuguese captains, were dangerous currents which they feared might stop them sailing home. The winds were wrong; the sun might turn them black; and anyway what was beyond the Cape? Nothing, they swore, but barren desert sand. Some feared that they might sail off the Earth's edge, and fall like stones into the depths of Hell.

Prince Henry, 'the Navigator', brother to the King, tried to breathe courage into his captains. He scoffed at frightened gossip, asking who could believe these silly sailors' yarns of death and danger waiting beyond the Cape? No one had been to see, so no one knew.

Gil Eannes, one of the younger men at Henry's court, responded to the challenge. Returning from his voyage to the south, he brought strange wild flowers, never seen before: picked, said the smiling captain, south of Cape Bojador.

Once that feared obstacle was overcome, the Portuguese with growing boldness sailed farther, beyond the Cape, along the coast of Guinea, and on south. Eventually their ships would find the way around the southern tip of Africa, into the Indian Ocean. But first, the Portuguese explored the western shores.

Why did they go? What were they looking for? They had no single cause, no simple quest. In their own minds they were Christ's soldiers and their King's, crusaders of a kind. Some of them, like Prince Henry, wondered what undiscovered lands might lie beyond the horizon: the urge to find out drove them

The Savage Trade

to the south. Other desires, more simple, were at work. New trade might make new fortunes. It was known that Africa provided fancy goods like ostrich feathers, ivory and, above all, gold, the metal for which men will fight and die.

Dreams of cheap gold, imported by the ton, did not come true, although some gold was shipped to Portuguese ports from West Africa. Instead, another kind of trade began.

The early voyages to Africa were all sent out under the royal command. In 1444 a man named Lançarote, a popular fellow at court in spite of his job as a tax collector, asked Prince Henry for permission to lead his own expedition to 'Guinea'. (The name then referred to land stretching from modern Senegal to Cameroun – the whole of West Africa.) Henry gave permission, in exchange for a one-fifth share of the profits of the voyage, and Lançarote sailed. He had six vessels, one of them commanded by Gil Eannes, the man who had broken the barrier of Cape Bojador eleven years before. Although caravels were rather small vessels, not much larger than a modern ocean-going yacht, this was the biggest expedition that had so far sailed to West Africa.

Unlike the leaders of the expeditions sent out by Prince Henry, Lançarote made no effort to explore. The caravels called at Heron Island, in Arguim Bay, and the sailors gorged themselves on young herons, which they killed by the dozen with a few swings of a club. There Lançarote addressed the whole company:

'My friends,' he said, 'we have left our land to do service to God and to the Prince, our lord. With such a fleet as we have, it would be a matter for shame if we return home without a worthy booty.'

The booty he was thinking of turned out to be human beings.

Lançarote had heard of an island, close to the mainland, where 200 people lived. He sent thirty men in small boats to spy out the land while the rest waited out of sight. The boats left in darkness, and as the dawn rose over the distant Sahara they came in sight of a village of huts by a beach.

They were not sure what to do. Lançarote had told them to

'That Miserable Company'

return to the caravels, but some were in favour of attacking the village at once. After some discussion, they decided to attack. Judging by the sudden commotion in the village, they had been spotted, and if they were to gain an advantage by surprise no time could be lost. They charged forward, yelling the names of Christian saints – their battle cries. The startled villagers quickly scattered. Frightened mothers forsook their children; fleeing husbands forgot their wives. Some were drowned as they tried to escape. Others hid in the huts, or under piles of seaweed, but the Portuguese soon found them and dragged them out. When the brief battle was over, the Portuguese had taken 165 prisoners – men, women and young children.

Thanking God for favouring them with this success, the raiders returned to their rendezvous with the caravels. During the next few days the Portuguese made several more raids on African villages. They were less successful, but when they reached their home port of Lagos in southern Portugal they had 235 Africans on board.

The Portuguese caravel was a vessel designed for coastal trade, but it proved capable of long Atlantic voyages.

The Savage Trade

The following day, at an early hour to avoid the hot August sun, the captives were led from the caravels to a field outside the walls of the town. There they were to be divided into five groups, so Prince Henry could choose the group he preferred. The rest were to be sold.

The early hour did not prevent many people coming to watch, from Lagos itself and from the country round about. Many of them had never seen Africans before, certainly not such a large number.

Among the spectators was Gomes Eannes de Azurara, who was the official court historian of Portugal and Keeper of the Royal Archives. He wrote a vivid description of this sale – the first big sale of African slaves in Europe.

It was impossible, said Azurara, not to feel sympathy for 'that miserable company' gathered in the field under the slanting rays of the early morning sun. Of course, these were pagans, non-believers. Yet, said Azurara, they were human beings too, and he hoped God would forgive him for shedding tears over pagans.

Many felt some pity. They felt also wonder at such an extraordinary sight. The captives were not all of the same people, for some were quite fair-skinned, some very black and some about as brown as mulattoes (people with one black and one white parent). It was the obvious distress of the captives that moved the chronicler. Some stood with lowered heads, their faces damp with tears. Some moaned miserably, and gazed up into the sky as if hoping help might come from there. Some struck their hands against their heads and threw themselves down upon the ground. Some sang a strange, sad chant like a funeral dirge.

To increase their suffering, there arrived upon the scene the officials whose job it was to divide the prisoners into five groups. To make an equal division, they paid no attention to families, but divided parents from children and husbands from wives. The job proved difficult. Desperately, people clung to each other. Mothers clasped their children in their arms and crouched on the ground, receiving heavy blows from those trying to part them but refusing to let go.

'That Miserable Company'

The difficulties of those in charge were aggravated by the presence of so many spectators, milling around without order or limit and anxious not to miss any part of the day's spectacle, for which they had left their fishing boats or their farms. Besides those humbler folk, there were nobles, courtiers, and Prince Henry himself, seated on a splendid horse and accompanied by his attendants. When at last the division had been made, and the Prince had received the forty-six people due to him, he quickly gave most of them away. He had no need of slaves himself. It was enough, he said, that so many souls, which had been lost before, could now be claimed for Christ. And certainly, as Azurara noticed, once the Africans had learned a little Portuguese they turned Christian without any fuss. (He did not wonder if these conversions owed more to common sense than religious faith.)

Those like Azurara who had felt such pity for the captured Africans consoled themselves with the belief that to be a Christian slave was far better than to be free but a pagan. And the fate of the Africans might have been – two centuries later would have been – much worse. The Portuguese treated them as they treated their own servants. Young boys were given an education in some craft. Those who seemed especially reliable were set free and perhaps given a little property. Eventually such men married Portuguese women. Young African women who were taken into service by rich Portuguese widows later received legacies from their former owners, enough to provide them with a dowry which attracted offers of marriage from Portuguese men.

Many Africans in Portugal also enjoyed a higher standard of living than they would have done back in Africa – better clothes, more varied food, weather-proof houses. In such things they were better off. Well-meaning Portuguese like Azurara took comfort from the feeling that, really, those who had captured the Africans on Lançarote's expedition had done them a good turn. It was the very argument still being used to justify slavery 400 years later.

The Savage Trade

The description of the first big European slave sale by Gomes Eannes de Azurara appears in his most famous work, The Chronicle of Guinea, *written in the Royal Library at Lisbon and finished on 18 February 1453. Although he wrote for the glory of Portugal and her royal family, Azurara was an accurate, truthful writer. But for his* Chronicle, *we should know little of early Portuguese voyages to West Africa.*

The Chronicle of Guinea *was translated into English by C. R. Beazely and Edgar Prestage and published in two volumes by the Hakluyt Society in 1896 and 1899.*

2

'AFRIC'S GOLDEN JOYS'

NORTH AFRICA, from Morocco to Egypt, had been closely linked with European civilization since ancient times. Relics of the Roman Empire can still be seen in Libya and Tunisia. But the rest of the huge continent of Africa, cut off by the barrier of

This is part of a map of Africa made for the King of France in 1375, showing towns and buildings that have disappeared. At bottom left is a boat with European sailors off the north-west African coast, and in the centre a desert nomad, or Tuareg, on his camel. But most interesting is the black king at bottom right. This is Mansa Musa, ruler of the large Mali empire in West Africa from 1307 to 1322. When he set out across the desert to visit Egypt, he took with him (it was said) 8,000 attendants and spent so much treasure that the price of gold in Egypt was severely reduced for many years.

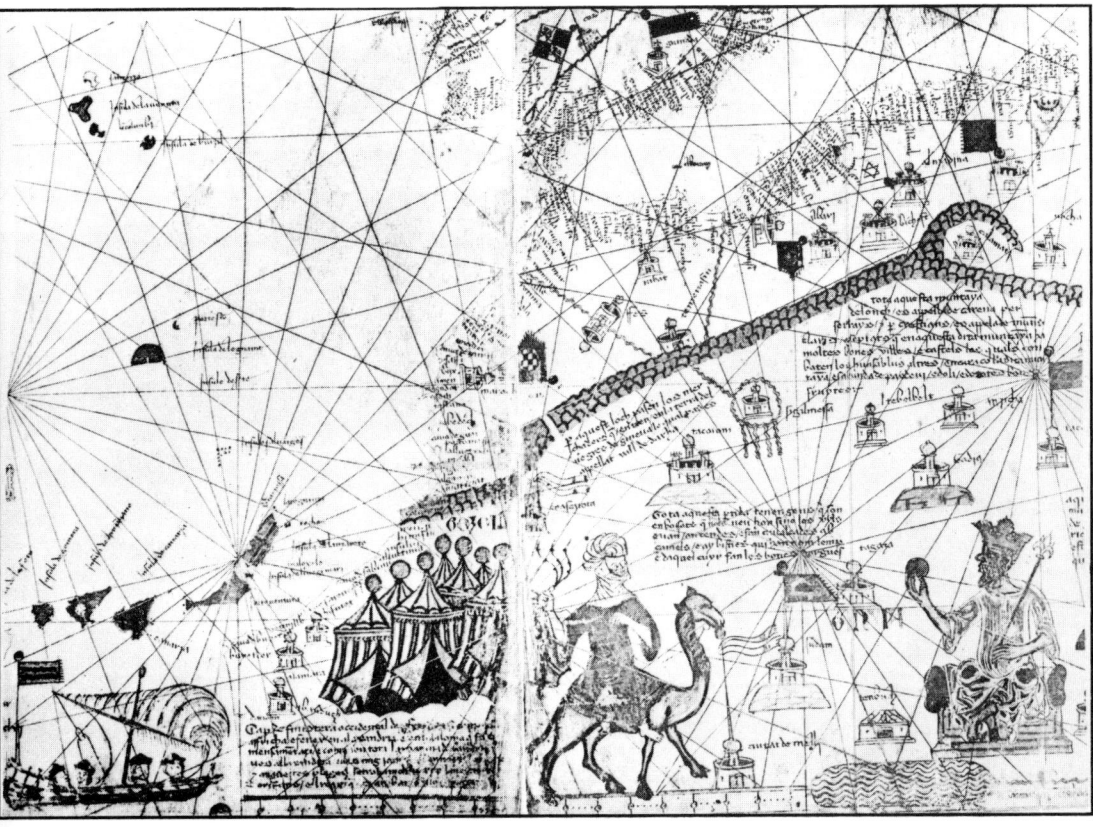

The Savage Trade

the Sahara Desert, remained almost unknown to Europeans until quite recent times.

In the fifteenth century North Africa became a battleground between Christians and Muslims. The Moors, a Muslim people from Morocco, had once ruled Portugal and still ruled part of Spain. But the Christians were gaining ground, and the Portuguese, having expelled the Moors from Portugal, pursued them across the straits of Gibraltar back to their North African homeland. Although they were unable to conquer Morocco, the Portuguese took and held the coastal stronghold of Ceuta. Once they had this foothold in Africa, their interest in the continent grew.

Among the news, gossip and rumour that the Portuguese picked up in North Africa, they grasped a few facts of special interest. In particular, they learned that the gold in circulation in Morocco came from beyond the Sahara, from lands outside the territory of Islam. This was good news to the Portuguese. If they could reach the land where the gold was mined, they might at the same time outflank Islam in the south. There was a legend of a mighty Christian king, Prester John, which had probably begun with some garbled story of the kingdom of Ethiopia, which was indeed Christian, though it was not the rich and powerful state pictured in the legend. The search for gold and the hope of outflanking the power of Islam by joining forces in a new crusade with the Christians of Prester John's kingdom – these ideas helped to drive the Portuguese caravels south along the coast of Africa.

Trade was another motive. Most of Europe's luxuries came from the East, brought by Muslim traders. The Portuguese, and others too, hoped to find a new route, by sea, to the markets of the East. Then they would be able to sail around the hostile Muslims and buy their 'spices' direct from the people who produced them. (When people spoke of 'spices' in the fifteenth century, they meant not only things like cloves and nutmeg, but also perfumes, sugar, even silks.)

The Portuguese, and later men of other European nations, had many reasons for sailing to Africa. But slave-trading was not one of them. Slaves were, and had been for centuries, one

'Afric's Golden Joys'

item of trade in Africa, but only a small item, never very important. The slave auction at Lagos after Lançarote's voyage, if not unique, was unusual because of the number of slaves sold. So large a sale was seldom seen at that time. Europeans had no great need for slaves in large numbers. They came to Africa in search of other things.

Unfortunately, other kinds of trade in Africa proved disappointing. Africa did have two products that Europeans wanted – gold and ivory. But they were small items, not the type of goods to fill many ships' holds. The Portuguese were at first pleased to find they could buy a grain called Malagueta pepper in West Africa, but once they had found the sea route to Asian markets they lost interest in the African product, which was coarser but no cheaper than the real pepper they could buy in the East. In spite of its gold, ivory and other products, including slaves, Africa was never so attractive to European merchants that they stopped searching for a route to the Far East.

In 1492 Christopher Columbus, sailing in the service of Spain, struck out across the Atlantic Ocean in search of a route west to Asia. Instead, he discovered the West Indies, then the

Christopher Columbus landing in the West Indies where he founded the first European empire in the Americas.

The Savage Trade

mainland of the two Americas. The new discoveries did not measure up to European dreams. The friendly, simple Arawak Indians of the Caribbean were nothing like the silk-clad Oriental merchants that Columbus had hoped to meet. Nevertheless, some of the rivers carried traces of gold.

When the Spaniards first arrived in the West Indies they found a peaceful, friendly people, the Taino Indians, who belonged to a group called the Arawaks. As the Europeans were quick to notice, they wore small ornaments of gold (but not the large objects shown in this engraving of 1613). The Spaniards dreamed of great gold mines, in which the hard work would be done by the Indians. 'How easy it would be,' they said, 'to convert these people – and to make them work for us.' True. They worked them so hard that the entire race died out.

'Afric's Golden Joys'

In their search for gold in the West Indies, the Spaniards used the native people as slave labourers. The Indians were not used to such work, and in captivity they soon sickened and died. After a few years they rebelled against Spanish rule, but they had no idea how to fight and in any case sticks and stones were no good against guns. The Spaniards, surprised and frightened by the revolt, slaughtered the Indians in hundreds.

At least one man was horrified by what was happening to the

Bartolomé de las Casas (1474–1566). A Spaniard who became a missionary, he was horrified by the savage treatment of the Indians by his fellow-countrymen. To save the Indians from the horrors of slave labour, he suggested bringing Africans to do the work, because he thought they would suffer less.

Caribbean Indians. He was a priest named Las Casas, who in 1517 went to plead at the Spanish court for the fast-disappearing people. Las Casas knew he had to be practical. The mines and plantations in the Spanish colonies needed labourers. If the local Indians were not employed, where was the labour to come from? Las Casas had a suggestion. He had seen a number of African slaves at work in the Spanish West Indies. They seemed to work well, without suffering in health or in spirit. He suggested that more Africans should be sent to the West Indies. Other people had also noticed that, while the local Indians were useless, Africans made good labourers. The King of Spain therefore issued a commission known as the *Asiento*, which allowed 4,000 Africans (later a larger number) to be taken to the New World. These slaves were to be provided by the Portuguese; soon the Portuguese slave markets were doing big business. The Atlantic slave trade had begun.

John Hawkins Cashes In

It soon became obvious that other European countries were going to want a share in this new trade. Portuguese threats did not discourage French traders – and pirates – from trespassing in West Africa, while from Plymouth in England came John Hawkins, looking for fame and fortune. He discovered that good profits could be made from taking Africans to sell as slaves to the Spanish colonies in the New World.

In 1567 Hawkins began his third and largest slaving expedition. He left Plymouth in early autumn in the *Jesus of Lubeck*, a big and clumsy 700-ton ship belonging to the Queen. He had five other vessels, and by the time he had finished his business

John Hawkins, a bold and intelligent Elizabethan adventurer and the first Englishman to adopt the slave trade as a serious business.

The Jesus of Lubeck, *Hawkins's flagship, a miniature painting from a manuscript. Hawkins borrowed her from the Queen, but she had been built in a Baltic port for the German merchants of the Hanseatic League and sold to King Henry VIII in 1545. By the time of Hawkins's voyage she was rather old-fashioned; her loss at San Juan de Ullua was no great blow to the English navy.*

ÆTATIS SVÆ LVIII
Anno Dmi 1591

in West Africa, he had picked up three or four more in the casual way of the sea – a caravel left abandoned by Portuguese fishermen, and a couple of French privateers who hoped for better pickings in Hawkins's company.

At first it looked as though Hawkins's plans might come to nothing. From an anchorage near Cape Verde, he led a party of 200 armed men ashore. Rowing with muffled oars under the cover of night, they approached a village a few miles inland, hoping to seize the unsuspecting inhabitants. When they reached the village they found it deserted, but the warm ashes of a fire proved that the inhabitants were not far away. Nearer than the Englishmen suspected, for suddenly there was an outbreak of fearful yells and arrows came flying out of the dark. Though surprised and outnumbered, the Englishmen in their helmets and leather jackets were little harmed by the unbarbed arrows, but they were forced to retire to their boats with only nine prisoners. Back on board they laughed about the incident – until those who had received slight flesh wounds from the arrows began to feel feverish, and the grim knowledge dawned that the arrows had been tipped with poison.

Eight men fewer, they sailed on looking for better luck. They seized seven small Portuguese ships lying at anchor in the hope, soon disappointed, that they were full of slaves. Other fights, with both Africans and Portuguese, resulted in only a few people captured and imprisoned in the ships' holds. One man gave himself up voluntarily to the English. He had been carrying on with one of the wives of a local king and thought that slavery under the whites was better than certain death.

When Hawkins's squadron assembled off Sierra Leone before setting out on the voyage across the Atlantic, he had only 150 slaves to sell instead of the 400 he had expected. The expedition seemed doomed to failure when two unexpected arrivals changed Hawkins's luck. They were a couple of local chiefs seeking help to attack their enemies in the nearby town of Conga. If the Englishmen would help them, their reward would be as many prisoners as they could fit into their holds.

Hawkins did not altogether like the prospects. He did not relish taking his ships up a river where they might be bottled up by Portuguese ships arriving on the coast. Besides, so far as he could understand from the difficult communications with the Africans – in a mixture of bad Portuguese and sign language – the battle ahead would be a big one: it seemed there were 6,000 warriors behind the wooden walls of Conga. However, in view of the emptiness of his holds, he agreed to fight.

While his allies attacked from one side, Hawkins advanced from the river on the other side. He had brought only small boats this far up river, but he had some ship's guns to bombard the stockade, which was made of tree trunks lashed together with creepers. The guns soon made a breach, but that was not a great help, as the last thing the English wanted was a hand-to-hand fight among packed paths and buildings inside the town. Surveying the buildings, all thatched with palm leaves, Hawkins ordered his bowmen to fire burning arrows into the thatch. Within minutes a large part of Conga was burning fiercely. The defenders fell back, the Africans attacking the other side of the town broke in, and a bloody slaughter began. Hawkins, seeing the battle was won, was intent on capturing as many prisoners as he could. As the smoke drifted away and the yells died down, he found to his satisfaction that he had about 250. It was as well for him that he took his own prisoners, for the slaves promised by the kings who hired him were not produced. Still, he had enough. Barrels were filled with fresh water and, as a helpful offshore wind sprang up, Hawkins led his squadron west into the Atlantic.

He sailed west and after six weeks land was sighted. Hawkins stopped at the green and mountainous isle of Dominica for water (what remained in his barrels had long ago turned flat and sour), but no colonists had yet settled in Dominica, so he headed for the northern coast of Venezuela on the mainland of South America – the 'Spanish Main'.

So far as the Spanish government was concerned, Hawkins was breaking several strict laws. He had no right to be in the Caribbean in the first place, and he had no right to trade with Spanish colonists, certainly not to sell them slaves: this right had been granted solely to the Portuguese. The colonists themselves looked at things differently, as Hawkins well knew. They were quite ready to buy from the English goods which were more expensive, or unobtainable, from licensed merchants.

Hawkins was prepared to be friendly or forceful. He was interested only in selling his slaves and getting home with the proceeds. At Margarita, where the Spaniards needed Africans to dive for pearls in the oyster beds, he was warmly received and stayed for eight days, buying and selling to the fifty Spaniards who lived there. At Borburata the governor refused permission to trade, but not in very strong language and without ordering the English to leave. For some time they remained in port, officially to clean weeds and barnacles off the ships' hulls but secretly carrying on their business.

At Rio de la Hacha the chief Spanish official was an old opponent of Hawkins and, instead of exchanging the usual polite letters, he and Hawkins exchanged gunfire. The English captured the town as the inhabitants fled and, by a piece of luck, some Spanish treasure, hidden nearby, fell into their hands. Hawkins did not want to ruin his reputation for honest trading, so he gave the treasure back, minus 4,000 gold pesos, an amount sufficient to pay for the sixty slaves he insisted on selling in Rio de la Hacha.

The hiding place of the treasure had been revealed by a Spanish slave who deserted to the English. When he left Rio de la Hacha, Hawkins handed this man over to the Spaniards, who hanged him for treason.

Some African captives, chained in the dark holds of Hawkins's ships, remained to be sold. At Santa Marta Hawkins arranged a little play-acting to make the governor's position easier. By previous agreement, he landed a party of armed men while his ships fiercely bombarded a particular building at the edge of the town, which had already been emptied of its contents. Trade then commenced. Later, the governor was able to report that the English had taken over his town by force.

Having sold most of his captives, Hawkins turned for home. Due to delays in West Africa and on the Main he was behind schedule, and the hurricane season was approaching. Off Cuba his fleet was caught in a severe storm which sprang dangerous leaks in his tired ships: live fish were coming through the gaps in the *Jesus of Lubeck*'s hull. Hawkins was forced to take shelter in the port of San Juan de Ullua, in Mexico. There he was trapped by a powerful Spanish war fleet. Though a truce had been agreed, the Spaniards attacked, and most of Hawkins's ships were destroyed or captured. He escaped and got back to England in one of the smaller ships, but for the time being the English left the slave trade alone.

Richard Jobson Refuses to Deal in People

Hawkins was not the only Englishman to deal in slaves in the reign of Elizabeth I, but he was the only slave trader on a large scale. In general, the English had a good reputation in West Africa. They were known as reasonably honest and peaceful traders, and were more popular than the Portuguese, but Hawkins's raids must have made many people think twice about entertaining the English.

Hawkins had no immediate imitators. After the attack at San Juan de Ullua relations between England and Spain grew less and less friendly, and eventually ended in full-scale war. It became impossible to trade with the Spanish colonies in an unofficial way, as Hawkins had, and as yet the English had no colonies of their own in the Caribbean and North America where they could sell slaves. In any case, many English people still felt that slave-dealing was unwise, if not immoral. Besides men like Hawkins, who felt no qualms about it, there were also men like Richard Jobson.

Jobson, who visited West Africa in 1620, was an agent of a merchant company trading with Africa. He was sent to the River Gambia in support of a trading expedition that had set out a year before, but when he arrived he found all the members of that expedition had died. Undaunted by this disaster, Jobson and his companions set off 300 miles up the Gambia to do some trading themselves.

They became friendly with an African merchant, Bucknor Sano, and instead of getting the hostile reception they had been warned to expect, they found themselves treated as welcome guests.

The trade Jobson was interested in was gold. He liked the Africans he met, but when it came to business he was as keen as any merchant to make the best bargain possible. He told his companions not to mention the subject of gold and to take no notice of the gold ornaments worn by the women. It was Bucknor Sano who brought the subject up. Noticing the gilt swords of the Englishmen, he asked if they were gold. Yes, they were, the English replied, seeming uninterested. 'It seems you have much of this in your country,' said Bucknor Sano. 'Oh yes, a great deal. Everyone uses it. If you happen to have any, we will buy it from you, seeing that we have more use for it than you.'

It is unlikely that Bucknor Sano was deceived by this pretended indifference. He could tell a good merchant's tale himself, and spoke airily of a distant city where the houses were roofed with solid gold tiles. At that the Englishmen could hardly conceal their excitement, but despite Bucknor Sano's promise to guide them there, somehow the journey never got started.

A sensible, humane man, Jobson strongly disapproved of the slave trade. When some people offered him slaves for sale, he refused. 'We are a people,' he explained, 'who do not deal in such commodities. We do not buy and sell one another, nor any creatures that bear human form. If you have no other kind of goods for sale, we will depart ...'

John Hawkins, a member of a famous family of Devon seafarers, was thirty-five at the time of his third slave-trading voyage. After the disaster of San Juan de Ullua he became Comptroller of the Navy, and his work helped to make the Navy fit to beat the Spanish Armada in 1588, when Hawkins commanded the reserves. He died at sea seven years later during an expedition against the Spanish West Indies.

Several men who took part in Hawkins's expedition of 1567 left an account of their experiences. They were printed by the tireless recorder of Elizabethan voyages, Richard Hakluyt, in The

'Afric's Golden Joys'

Principal Navigations . . . of the English Nation, *first published in 1589 and enlarged in later editions. An inexpensive edition was published in the Everyman series (London, 1927), in eight volumes. See also Rayner Unwin's* The Defeat of John Hawkins *(Allen & Unwin, London 1960).*

Richard Jobson published his enthusiastic book about West Africa, The Golden Trade, *in 1623. Some long extracts are printed in* West African Explorers, *edited by C. Howard and J. H. Plumb (World's Classics, Oxford University Press, 1951).*

In spite of Jobson's optimistic reports, his company was unwilling to risk any more money on expeditions to West Africa. It seems that Jobson, who never lost his eagerness to go back, did later set out on a new voyage to the Gambia, but there is no record that he ever arrived.

3
KINGDOMS AND VILLAGES

THE reason why Africans made better slave labourers than the Indians of the West Indies and North America was that they came from a more advanced type of society. The people of the West Indies, who greeted the first Spaniards with flowers and were repaid with forced labour and death, were simple food gatherers who had not reached that stage in civilization when man learns to grow crops and keep animals. The Spaniards of Columbus's time were as alien to them as creatures from another planet. Their language, their ideas, their customs – all were incomprehensible to the Indians. Forced to become a part of this strange new society, to sacrifice their freedom and to work all day long under harsh discipline, they simply grew sick and died.

The people of West Africa, however, were much closer to the Europeans. Most of them were farmers. (There were also hunters and fishermen and even some tribes of food-gatherers in the rain forest; these people, like the Indians, did not make useful slaves.) Many West Africans were skilled craftsmen, and the European colonist who bought a slave often found that he had bought not just an unskilled labourer fit only for simple tasks in the field, but a capable iron-worker, or a miner, or someone who knew more than he did about growing crops in tropical conditions.

In the Sahel, the interior of West Africa, large empires had risen, ruled and fallen since the time when the Normans were conquering England. First Ghana, then Mali (no relation to the modern states with those names) had spanned a territory the size of France. When the Portuguese arrived in West Africa, a third Sahel empire, the Songhai Empire, was still at the height of its influence. But because they never travelled far inland,

A figure in bronze of a Portuguese soldier, made by a West African artist in the late sixteenth century.

African craftsmen working iron: the man on the left is operating bellows to fan the furnace, the man on the right is hammering the iron on an anvil. The blacksmith's trade had a touch of magic about it, and blacksmiths commanded great respect in African villages. This engraving comes from an old account by a European missionary.

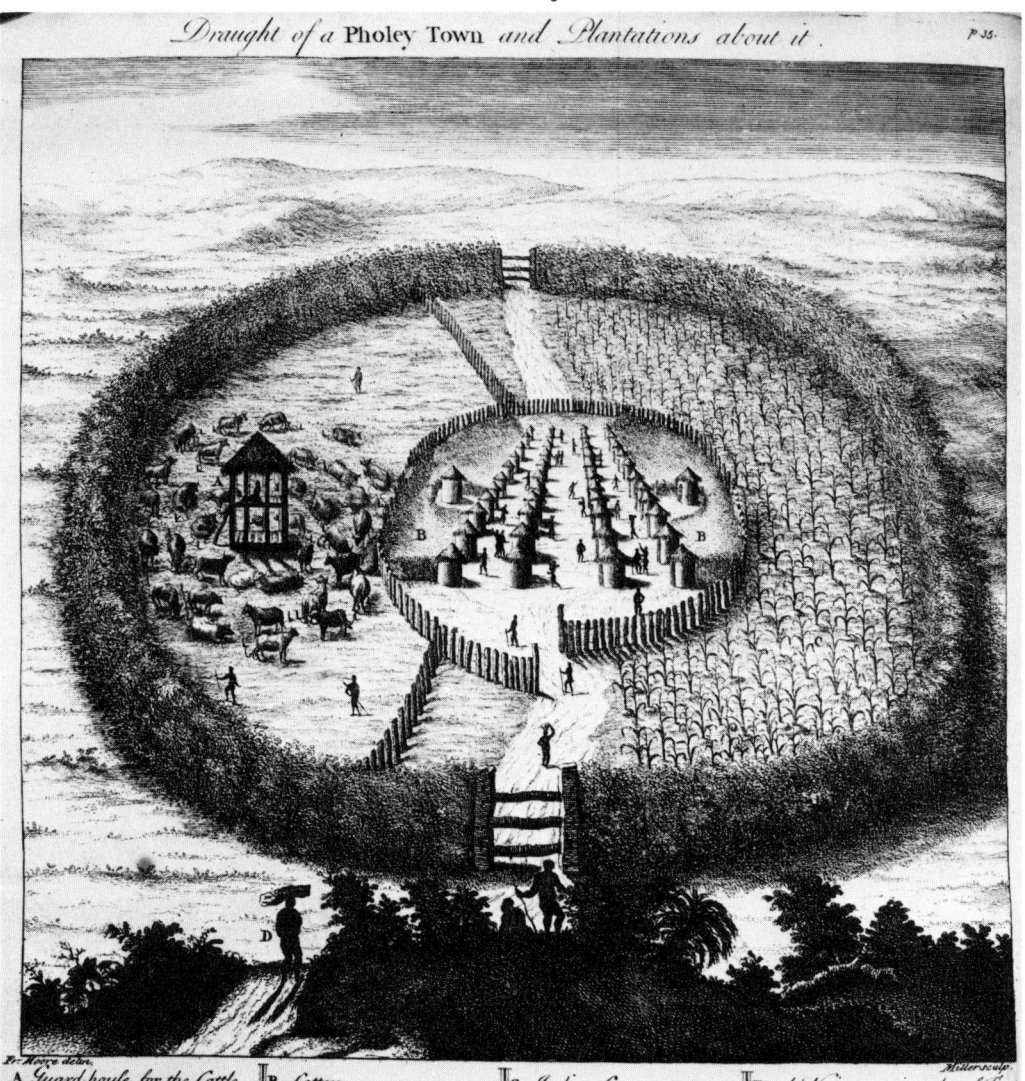

An African town, drawn by Francis Moore for his book Travels into the Inland Parts of Africa *(1738). At the left are the cattle, with a guardhouse (A) for the herdsman. Cotton is grown (B) near the houses and 'Indian corn' (maize or sweetcorn) at the right. The whole place is surrounded by a prickly fence, entered by two barred gates.*

Kingdoms and Villages

the Portuguese knew nothing of it except what they heard through the gossip of the market and the whispers of the savanna.

In Guinea itself (the coastal region from Senegal to Cameroun) the African states were smaller. Often there was only one town of any size, surrounded by a wall which would also shelter the people of the surrounding villages if the state were attacked. People lived in large family units around a central palace occupied by the king and his numerous family. Each day they went out to work in the fields, returning to their homes before dusk.

The towns and villages of West Africa were linked by trade routes which ran from the coast through forest and savanna, and a few of these crossed the Sahara to North Africa. Cowrie shells, which were widely used as coins, were common in

Small cowrie shells, kept on a string or in a leather bag, were used as money in many parts of Africa. They were sometimes given as change for European coins.

Guinea although they came all the way from islands in the Indian Ocean, via Egypt and across the desert.

There were regular markets for local trade. Each market drew people from a wide area, for market days were staggered so that nearby towns would not compete against each other for customers. It was a general rule of the country that even in war-time no one should interfere with women going to market. A man walking into a strange village might be in danger, but a woman with an earthenware pot or a bundle of vegetables on her head might pass unhindered. Pots could be traded for oil or fish, salt, pepper or dried cassava (a starchy root). A great deal of haggling and joking went on among the hundreds of women, old and young, who came regularly to the market as their mothers and grandmothers had done before them.

The early European arrivals in West Africa saw little of how African society was run, either because they were not interested or because for them, stuck in their ships on the coast, there was little to see. One of the few states that was visited by Europeans early on was the state of Benin, in what is now Nigeria.

A visitor entering Benin about 1600 found himself in a city the size of Bordeaux. A wide unpaved street stretched for several kilometres without bend or corner. Houses built of red clay polished until it looked like marble lined each side. The thatched roofs were open to the sky at the centre to let out smoke and let in light, for the houses had no windows. An earth wall three metres high surrounded the city. The palace of the king, or Oba, was almost a town in itself. It was a maze of courts and chambers and long galleries, with pillars sheathed in copper and walls decorated with works of art in bronze.

Some Portuguese visited Benin as early as 1472. Before they were received by the Oba, sitting on his ivory throne beneath a canopy of silk, they had to be thoroughly washed, and when they entered his presence they had to lie flat on their faces. The Oba, though treated as a god, was friendly. He gave the Portuguese permission to trade in his dominion, and later paid them the compliment of taking a Portuguese woman as one of his wives. The Portuguese did not doubt that they were meet-

Kingdoms and Villages

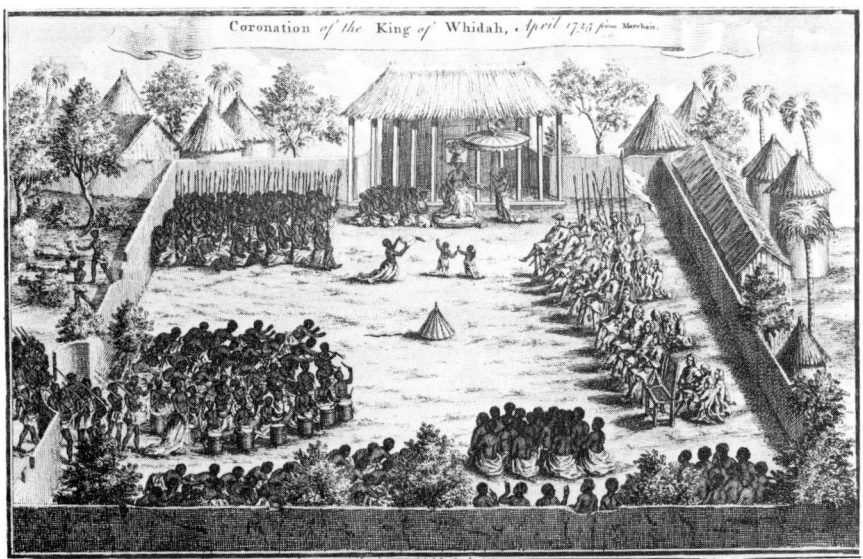

The scene at Whydah, or Ouidah, west of Lagos, at the coronation of the local king in 1725. Ouidah was then becoming an important centre for the slave trade, especially for the French.

ing a great monarch. They did not think of him as the illiterate chief of a savage tribe, the kind of mistake that many Europeans were to make in later times.

At first the Portuguese treated African rulers, like the Oba of Benin or the King of Kongo, as equals. Several minor rulers in Africa visited Portugal and were well received. One hundred years later prejudice had set in, and a missionary from the Kongo kingdom could write with astonishment and disgust that the people there 'think themselves the foremost men in the world, and nothing will persuade them to the contrary . . . They imagine that Africa is not only the greatest part of the world, but also the happiest and most agreeable.' Words almost failed him when he came to describe the beliefs of the king of Kongo himself. 'He is persuaded,' wrote this outraged European, 'that there is no other monarch in the world who is his equal, or exceeds him in power or wealth.' In other words, he behaved just like (for example) the King of France.

In many parts of Africa, people had good reason to feel pleased with themselves. At the end of the period known in

Europe as the Middle Ages, certain societies in West Africa were, in some ways, no less advanced than Western Europe. It is true that there were some important things lacking. Most African languages had never gained a written form, so there was no 'literature' or 'history' in a European sense. And, another example, that useful object the wheel had not been invented in Africa south of the Sahara. The first Europeans confronted the Africans with many things that they could not understand – even their ships were bewildering objects. The only 'ships' known in Africa were canoes, and the Portuguese vessels were not recognized as 'ships' at all. Some Africans thought they were large birds; others, seeing them with their sails furled, thought they must be some kind of gigantic fish; a third theory was that they were ghosts. Although the Africans were neither so backward nor so different from themselves as Europeans came to believe, to a Portuguese, or French, or English sailor arriving in West Africa in the seventeenth century, it still seemed a very strange place.

The scenery alone appeared frightening. The forest, dense and forbidding, was more black than green, and strangely silent. Vast swamps stretched endlessly along coasts and rivers, where the mangroves formed an amphibious jungle, a place of secret holes and caverns among slimy black roots. In those surroundings it was easy to feel, all around, the presence of spirits, human and inhuman, good and evil. Spirits which sometimes had to be appeased with tributes guarded a particular tree, or grove, or a river pool. West African spiritual life, with its priestesses and witch doctors, its endless dancing and – to European ears – weird music, its charms, fetishes and taboos, was puzzling and peculiar to Europeans. Most of them dismissed it as ignorant barbarity.

Africans had a different attitude to life; what was natural to them was strange to Europeans, and vice versa. Africans had very little of that searching curiosity which was one of the reasons why Europeans came to Africa, not Africans to Europe. They were not driven by the urge that made Europeans risk hardship, pain and death in search of land or gold or knowledge. When David Livingstone was searching for the

Kingdoms and Villages

Europeans saw many curious sights in Africa, and they were not always skilful at describing – or drawing – them. This is a picture of a hippopotamus, or 'sea horse', as it appeared to a European traveller in the seventeenth century.

And here is a 'camel-leopard', actually a giraffe, a creature that filled Europeans with astonishment. Obviously this artist could not believe the evidence of his eyes when it came to drawing the long thin neck.

source of the Nile in 1868, an African chief told him: 'We let the streams run on, and do not inquire whence they rise or whither they flow.'

Although Africans seemed, and were, a more easy-going people, they had laws and rules of behaviour which were no less strict than European laws. In most African societies adultery was a serious crime punished by death, though otherwise capital punishment was less common than in Europe. Arab travellers who visited certain West African states before the Europeans arrived found that strangers could move from place to place with no fear of robbery or violence. Not all parts were so peaceful, but when the slave trade became a profitable business, no one was safe anywhere on the road.

Not understanding African society, Europeans usually thought the worst and, secure in their own ignorance, treated African customs with contempt. Slavery encouraged this attitude. For if Africans were no better than miserable savages, then it was easier to justify making them slaves.

Most Europeans believed that all Africans were cannibals, or would be cannibals if they had the chance. In reality, cannibalism was very rare, though this long-standing European error was encouraged by Africans themselves, who were usually ready to accuse their enemies of cannibalism. Of course, Africans had the same strange ideas about Europeans too. One of the terrors of being sold into European slavery was the certain belief that you would be eaten by the 'white devils'.

Rosehall, a magnificent plantation house in Jamaica which has been recently restored. At one time it was owned by a Mrs Annie Palmer, who is said to have been so cruel to her slaves that they finally murdered her.

4

THE TYRANT SUGAR

For many years most slaves bought by Europeans in West Africa went to the Spanish colonies in America; but during the seventeenth century the English, the French, the Dutch and even the Danes gained colonies of their own in the Caribbean. French colonists on Guadeloupe, English on Barbados, Dutch on Curaçao, all wanted cheap African labour – slaves – to work their plantations. The numbers were small at first; but as the colonies grew so did the demand for slaves.

During the second half of the seventeenth century, the demand began to grow much faster. What caused it was a change, on West Indian plantations, to a new crop – sugar. Before this, sugar had been an uncommon luxury in Europe, grown only in a few places near the Mediterranean, but, once it began to come in from the West Indies, sweet-toothed

Harvesting the cane under the eye of white supervisors armed with whip and pistol. A nineteenth-century engraving.

Europeans learned to eat it in large quantities. It was as though caviare became as common as fishcakes; by 1700 sugar was by far the biggest product of the West Indies. Many a planter grew rich on sugar, including some who never visited their plantations but lived in comfort in London or Paris while their managers ran the plantations. Larger fortunes were made by private citizens than ever before. People spoke of someone being 'as rich as a West Indian' in the way that today we might say 'rich as an oil sheikh'. There was an estate in Barbados which was valued at about £400 in 1640. Then the owner changed over to sugar-planting, and a few years later he sold the estate for £7,000.

Sugar was not an easy crop to grow. Its main drawback was that it was what a modern economist would call 'labour-intensive'; in other words it required a very large number of human workers. In order to make their enormous profits, the planters had to have labour which was both plentiful and cheap. The answer – the *only* answer it seemed to them – was to be found in West Africa. Sugar planting and the slave trade went hand in hand. 'There is nothing that does more to help the growth of these [West Indian] colonies', the French government announced in 1670, than 'the trade of Negroes from Guinea to the Islands.'

It led to growth in Europe too. Profits made out of slaves and sugar created the wealth which helped pay for the great economic leap forward in Britain known as the Industrial Revolution.

There was more than one way to make a fortune out of the sugar plantations without being a sugar-grower or a slave-trader. A man named William Miles came to Bristol in the eighteenth century with one and a half pence in his pocket, took a labouring job until he had saved up £15, then signed on as ship's carpenter in a vessel sailing to America. When he arrived there he used his savings to buy a couple of barrels of sugar, which he brought back to Bristol with him and sold for a very large profit. With the profit from the sale of the sugar he bought English manufactured goods, such as clothes and tools, which he sent for sale in the West Indies, taking payment in

Sugar barrels being unloaded at Bristol, about 1800.

sugar. The sugar he resold in Bristol at the usual fat profit, which in turn enabled him to buy more manufactured goods to sell to the planters. The process continued, with profits accumulating and the business rapidly expanding. In time William Miles died, leaving a son, also a good businessman, to take over. By the time the son died, the property of the Miles estate was valued at over half a million pounds.

Not everyone connected with sugar made a fortune. The sugar crop was subject to many disasters – drought, hurricanes, disease, not to mention war, which was as common as peace in the West Indies. Sugar took fifteen months to grow,

The Tyrant Sugar

Slaves planting sugar cane in the West Indies. On a typical Barbados plantation in the seventeenth century, the working day in the fields lasted from 6 a.m. to 6 p.m., with a two-hour break at midday.

twice as long as other tropical crops like tobacco, and it required not only more workers but also more equipment: copper boilers, pipes, cooling pots, and so on.

First the land had to be cleared and ploughed, then divided into squares of about one metre. Holes six inches (15 centimetres) deep were dug for the plants, a back-breaking task for the lines of slaves who moved slowly across the field, row by row, with the whips of the overseers hovering over them. At harvest time the cane was cut with little sickles, stripped and topped like a leek, tied in bundles, and loaded on to donkeys to be carried to the mill (the donkeys were trained to find their way from field to mill without being led).

The sugar was extracted from the canes in the mill by a long and clumsy process. First the cane was crushed between heavy rollers (which sometimes also crushed the fingers of the men feeding in the cane). The juice was drained off and carried by pipes to the boiling house, where it was boiled down to a syrup. In the boilers the scum that formed on the top had to be skimmed off with ladles, a tricky job. The liquid passed through five or six great copper boilers before it was finally transferred in huge ladles to the cooler, where the sugar crystallized. Working in the boiler house was extremely unpleasant. The stench, like sickly-sweet manure, was filthy, and the heat terrific. Limbs swelled in the hot, damp atmosphere, and even the strongest slaves, specially picked for the job, could not work in the boiler house for more than four hours at a time.

The slaves existed for nothing except work. They lived in huts and ate poor food – mushy porridge and dried fish were a common diet – apart from what they produced in their own patches. Not all were cruelly treated, but many suffered savage and horrible punishments. They had no right to appeal against their owners as they were not protected by the law. (In the French colonies they were – in theory – protected by the rules

The scene inside the boiling house. The juice from the crushed canes was boiled in great copper boilers, creating a sickly, steamy atmosphere in which the ladling process went on, in shifts, day and night.

The Tyrant Sugar

On many plantations, like this one in Brazil, slaves were savagely punished for the slightest fault. Such pictures, published in Europe, helped to arouse public opinion against slavery.

of the *Code Noir*, but the rules were not often enforced.) Worst of all, they had nothing in life to look forward to. They were condemned to a life of endless toil, and their children after them, and their grandchildren, to eternity.

5

KINGS AND CABOCEERS

ALTHOUGH Europeans discovered West Africa half a century before Columbus discovered America, the interior of the continent remained unknown until the nineteenth century. The French ventured a few hundred miles up the Senegal and the English up the Gambia, but nowhere else in West Africa did Europeans go far inland. They had been visiting and trading in the network of creeks and rivers which they called the Oil Rivers for five hundred years before it dawned on them that this was the delta of the great River Niger, whose outlet had always been a mystery.

The appearance of the region, with its desert and dense forest, was not attractive to Europeans. Uglier still were the deadly tropical diseases that infested the land.

A river scene in West Africa. To Europeans, the dense growth of the rain forest was strange and forbidding.

Kings and Caboceers

> Beware and take care
> Of the Bight of Benin,
> There's few that comes out
> Though many goes in.

The sailors' song on the old Guinea ships was grim but true. Before quinine was discovered as a cure for malaria, Europeans in West Africa died as easily as the humming mosquitoes which, unknown to them, brought death in their sting, or the nasty little jet-styled tsetse flies, carriers of sleeping sickness.

A more serious obstacle to Europeans than African jungles, deserts or fevers was the attitude of the African people. When Europeans decided to establish colonies in Africa near the end of the nineteenth century, they were able to do it because of their greater strength and fire-power. In the eighteenth century they were not so powerful, and the Africans were able to keep Europeans out of their country (something the Indians of North America had not been able to do).

In 1758 a British Member of Parliament suggested that Britain should buy the land in Guinea where the gold mines lay. To the officials of the Board of Trade, who knew the real situation in West Africa, the idea was ridiculous. They explained why. British interests in Guinea – that is, British trade and British possessions – depended chiefly if not entirely on the good will and friendship of the Africans. Even those tiny possessions the British had – a dozen little trading posts dotted along the coast like raindrops clinging to a window sill – were only permitted by the local people on payment of an annual rent. As for gold mines, you might as well try to buy the moon. All attempts to discover anything about the interior of the country, especially the gold mines, had run into solid African opposition. Europeans were welcome only as long as they kept to their trading posts. Inland, they were not admitted.

One of the difficulties that Europeans discovered when they did try to move into Africa was the large number of independent states they had to deal with. Each little state was suspicious of its neighbours, if not actually at war with them, and that made movement from one state to another slow and difficult, sometimes impossible. The traveller who made himself welcome in one place was for that very reason treated as a likely enemy when he travelled a few miles farther into the territory of a different ruler.

The slave trade itself helped the growth of petty states along the Guinea coast, especially in the region of the Niger delta. Most of these states consisted of one sordid little town, a few outlying villages, and nothing more. They existed for a single purpose, the slave trade, doing business as middlemen between the African suppliers farther inland and the European buyers on the coast. The states of the delta, although they might be rivals in trade, sometimes co-operated with each other against outside enemies. Though so small, they were stronger than they appeared. They controlled not only the export trade in slaves, but also the import trade in European goods, and the largest item in that trade was – guns. The slave trade brought firearms to Africa, and power to those who first possessed them.

The slave trade had become a joint Afro-European enterprise. Although a few European slave-dealers organized kidnapping raids in the eighteenth century, the days of armed expeditions like those of John Hawkins were over. The European buyers in their ships and factories depended on the Africans on the coast for their supply of slaves. The coastal people in turn bought slaves from inland states (mainly prisoners of war or convicted criminals), but they also captured their own on military expeditions against their neighbours. Being better armed, they were able to attack peaceful villages without great danger to themselves; they were also able to hold their own if attacked by the much larger states of the interior. For hundreds of miles inland from the coast, violence and disorder became the common condition of society, with petty kings waging war on the smallest excuse, or no excuse at all, in order to take prisoners whom they could sell as slaves on the coast.

Francis Moore, a factor (trade representative) for the Royal African Company on the Gambia in the early eighteenth century, explained how one of these slave-trading rulers went about his business.

Guns were the most desirable of European trade goods. At a British post in West Africa, Africans gleefully test their new weapons. From a book published in 1824.

Hearing of the arrival of a slave ship, 'the king goes and ransacks some of his enemies' towns, seizing the people and selling them for such commodities as he is in want of, which commonly is brandy or rum, gunpowder, ball, guns, pistols and cutlasses for his attendants and soldiers; and coral and silver for his wives . . . In case he is not at war with any neighbouring king, he then falls upon one of his own towns, which are numerous, and uses them in the same manner.'

The Europeans – the captains of the slave ships or the

factors in the coastal trade stations – depended for their supply of slaves mainly on petty rulers of this kind. The African slave-trading kings and 'caboceers' (African traders; the word comes from the Portuguese and means 'head man') were as crafty as any horse-dealer. In spite of the scornful European belief that Africans were ignorant creatures who would stupidly trade away gold for trinkets, they often got the better of the bargain. There was one French captain who bought a large quantity of gold and sailed home congratulating himself on having made a fortune in exchange for his trashy trade goods, only to discover when he arrived that he had actually bought a worthless load of old brass filings.

According to the French merchant Jean Barbot, who spent some time on the Gold Coast in the late seventeenth century, the people there had at first been easily swindled because it never entered their thoughts that white men would cheat them. They soon learned better, and became as careful as an old lady buying vegetables in a French market. They would measure metal bars against the soles of their feet, they would taste rum or brandy to see if it had been watered, they would examine every kettle and basin for cracks as strictly as Europeans examined the people they bought as slaves. They even learned to tell whether Dutch cloth had been dyed at Leiden or at Haarlem.

Both sides cheated when they could, and as the trade was such a rough, unregulated business – no Office of Fair Trading here – crude bargaining, blackmail and deceit were more common than honest dealing. The Europeans were often in the weaker position. It was the custom to buy the king's slaves first, then those of the chief caboceer, and so on in order of importance. The king might offer slaves who were old or sick, but the traders could not reject them if they hoped to trade with anyone else. The caboceers were adept at concealing the symptoms of age or illness in their slaves. They would generally shave their heads to make it more difficult to judge age, and rub down their bodies with palm oil to make them look sleek and muscular.

The Europeans sometimes benefited from the willingness of

caboceers to cheat their king, or each other. Wily traders invited the captains to visit them at night, when they would sell slaves outside the quota agreed with the king and without payment of the tax due to the king on each slave sold.

Most of the caboceers on the Guinea coast in the eighteenth century are unknown to history even by name. Many of them were of mixed race – African mother, European father – and were baptized Christians, able to speak one or more European languages. A few had visited Europe. There was a powerful caboceer at the big English trading station of Cape Coast Castle who was said to have an English wife, besides numerous African wives. Other African traders picked up European customs through their long contact with the whites, although their ideas of gracious living in Europe, being based on what they saw on merchant ships, were rather strange. A certain Grandy King George, who lived in Old Calabar, wrote to a Liverpool merchant in the 1770s with a list of the trade goods he required. Among them were a looking glass, a blue coat with gold lace, an armchair, a case of razors, a gold-mounted cane, and a close-stool (an old type of lavatory seat). These were the kind of articles that might be seen in the cabin of a European ship's master. They were strange innovations in West Africa.

The English and the Queen of Auguina

One of the local rulers on whose good will the English merchants depended in the early eighteenth century was the Queen of Auguina, who ruled a small kingdom on the Gold Coast. This lady, like the English Queen Elizabeth I, was unwilling to share her power with a husband, so she never married. She was no Virgin Queen however. She had many lovers, it was said, but they were all slaves, who could never become rivals to the throne.

The Queen of Auguina allowed the English to build a fort on her territory at Winneba. It was a large building, said to have cost £10,000—a huge sum then. Winneba was usefully placed for ships from England. It was on a river mouth which provided fresh water, and near forests which provided timber

for ship repairs. It also had a good supply of oysters, whose shells were used as building material; but, most important, it allowed contact with the inland kingdom of Akim, an important source of gold and slaves.

The Queen of Auguina, though friendly to the English, saw no reason why she should not fry two fish in the same pan. The Dutch, she knew, were jealous of the English fort at Winneba and eager to cut in on the trade with Akim. One way or another, the Queen got in touch with the Dutch and suggested they might like to build a trading station at another place on her territory, not far from Winneba.

A hint of these negotiations reached English ears, causing anger and dismay at Winneba. There was some hot-headed talk of an armed expedition against the Queen, but more experienced men advised diplomacy. A local chief was brought in as peace-maker, no doubt receiving presents from the English for his efforts on their behalf. The Queen let it be

The British fort at Winneba, in the territory of the Queen of Auguina, 1727.

known that she was willing to throw out the Dutch – for a price. After some polite discussion, the price turned out to be a couple of cases of strong liquor and a quantity of English cloth. The goods were handed over, the Dutch were ordered to depart, and the English trade to Akim was preserved from interlopers.

A Slave Raid

In 1765 an English sailor named Isaac Parker deserted his ship while she was lying at the slaving port of Old Calabar on the Cross River (now in Nigeria). He was given shelter by the son of a local ruler, Dick Ebro, and stayed with him nearly six months. He spent most of his time hunting and fishing, for things were quiet at Old Calabar. There had been peace in the

The Savage Trade

country up river for some time, and as a result the miserable processions of chained captives arriving for sale had stopped. Slaves, Parker observed, were in short supply.

One day his host came to him and said, 'Parker, will you go to war with me?' Parker shrugged. 'I don't mind,' he replied, and set to work cleaning swords and repairing the muskets supplied by European traders – shoddy weapons made only for the African trade, but greatly prized in Africa.

The raiding party set out in big war canoes, each with guns

Slave-raiders attacking a village, from a print published in 1809.

Captured villagers on their way to be sold at the coast.

capable of firing two-pound shot mounted in the bow and stern. They paddled slowly along the little creeks that wound through the swampy country beyond the coast. At dusk they approached a village. The canoes were dragged up on the bank and one or two men left on guard, while the rest crept up on the village. A swift rush in the darkness, and a dozen terrified people were seized and handcuffed, while the rest scattered. The raiders returned to their canoes in high spirits at the success of their raid. They forced their captives to lie in the bottom of the canoes, and set off for the next village.

The raid was repeated at three or four places, the raiders

lying up during daylight under cover of bushes. When they returned to Old Calabar they had 45 prisoners, men, women and children. The prisoners were chained in the slave pens until sold to the slave ships. Families were separated, except for infants still feeding at the breast who were allowed to stay with their mothers.

Not long afterwards Parker took part in another expedition, farther up the river, with the same result. It was rare for a European to witness these events; but similar raids, unrecorded, took place continually up and down the coast.

A Crafty Caboceer

Early in the eighteenth century, the Royal African Company had a ramshackle trading station called Fort Commenda on the Gold Coast. The Company's factor there was William Baillie, or Brainie, and the most powerful caboceer in the district was a man named John Cabess, or Kabes. Crafty and unreliable, Cabess was the bane of the factor's life. His loyalty to the Company which employed him was, to say the least, doubtful, yet his influence was so great that Baillie could not do without him.

One day Cabess came into the fort, complaining loudly as usual, along with some African traders from up country. Cabess told Baillie that these men had a couple of slaves, but he could hardly believe they were seriously interested in selling them as they had asked the high price of six ounces of gold each. He had seen the slaves and had told the traders that he would give no more than four ounces (which as Cabess well knew was the top price paid by the Company at that time). Baillie was annoyed that Cabess had been bargaining with the Company's money without his knowledge, but after ticking him off he agreed to buy the slaves at four ounces each in order to preserve Cabess's reputation among the traders.

When the two slaves arrived, they proved to be sad old men who, in the eyes of the Company, were certainly not worth the agreed price. Baillie was very angry with Cabess and suspected that, not for the first time, he was organizing some underhand deal. He told the traders that the slaves were not worth buying, but asked them privately to come and see him again when John Cabess had gone. Later, when they returned, he discovered by questioning them that they had originally agreed to sell the slaves at less than half the price Cabess had said. The surplus, needless to say, would have gone into the caboceer's pocket.

He pulled this trick more than once. Sometimes he would dress up some of his own men, choosing those whom Baillie did not know by sight, and pretend they were slavers from the north. Watched by the suspicious factor, he would bargain hard and long with the 'traders' (whose language, of course, Baillie could not speak) and end by paying a rather high price for their slaves. What Baillie did not know, though he might suspect something of the sort, was that the slaves were already Cabess's property, since he had bought them from genuine northern traders a few days before, paying for them with goods taken from the Company warehouse (without permission). He was, in effect, reselling to the Company its own slaves, and at a price, needless to say, much higher than that paid to the traders. Baillie often felt like the man who lent his walking stick to another and then found himself being hit over the head with it.

What made John Cabess, and others like him, indispensable to the European factors, apart from their local influence and their contacts with the interior kingdoms, was the simple fact that in the slave trade demand was nearly always greater than supply. We seldom hear of slave pens full of slaves awaiting a buyer, but often of ships unable to fill their holds, and of factors casting about desperately to find a new source of slaves. John Cabess had no need to worry about the threats and reprimands of the English factor at Fort Commenda because he knew that next week or the week after the factor would be urgently entreating him to do all he could to find more slaves, even if he had to pay a higher price than usual. And when, as sometimes happened, the factor stood firm against some outrageous demand by Cabess, such as full payment for a slave who was obviously dying, the wily caboceer would sell him to an 'inter-

European slave-traders examining a man offered for sale, while his captors bargain over the price.

loper' (an independent slaver, not belonging to the Company), who would usually pay a better price.

John Cabess was a thorn in the side of the English. The thorn caused constant pain, but if it were pulled out, the body would bleed to death. 'I am afraid,' sighed Mr Baillie, 'that the Company trade will never flourish until his end comes.' The only consolation he could think of was that Cabess was old and beginning to grow feeble. He could not, Baillie thought hopefully, live much longer.

John Cabess seems to have lived longer than Baillie hoped, though we do not know exactly when he died. Like many other minor characters in the history of the slave trade, he makes one or two brief appearances and then vanishes. The diary kept by William Baillie at Fort Commenda between 1714 and 1718, now in the London Public Records Office, records his dealings with Cabess. Parts of it are printed in Elizabeth Donnan's Documents Illustrative of the History of the Slave Trade to America *(4 volumes, Washington, D.C., 1930–35, reprinted 1965), which contains the reports of many other incidents in this book.*

A peaceful scene in a West African village, with women cooking and pounding flour while the men sit around talking. This is actually a village in Ashanti, in what is now Ghana, but probably the village of Olaudah Equiano looked something like this.

6

'AN END TO HAPPINESS'

In the Ibo village of Essaka, east of the River Niger, Olaudah Equiano was born about 1745. As he remembered it many years later, Essaka was a pretty little village, set in a glade near the edge of the forest, with many trees bearing exotic fruit, but since then the name Essaka has disappeared from the map and we do not know exactly where the village was. Although the people had heard of Benin, and vaguely thought of the Oba of Benin as their overlord, they had never seen a white man. As there were plenty of Europeans on the coast at that time, and occasionally some at Benin, Essaka must have been off the beaten track and a long way from the sea.

Olaudah's father had a mark running across his forehead, a long scar made deliberately by cutting away a flap of skin and rubbing it into a ridge. This marked him as one of the village elders, or magistrates. Olaudah was the youngest of seven children, all boys except one, and as often happens to the youngest child, he was the pet of the family, his mother's favourite.

Life in the eighteenth-century Ibo village was simple. There were few luxuries, yet the people were no worse off than farm labourers in Europe at the same period. Men and women dressed alike, in a kind of cotton kilt. The material was made in the villages and often dyed a bright blue with the juice of berries growing in the neighbourhood. Wives of the chief men wore gold ornaments; the higher their rank the more numerous the ornaments, so that very grand ladies had some difficulty walking because of the heavy bangles jangling on their ankles.

As in other parts of Africa, the women did more than a fair share of the work. It was the women who spun and wove cloth, and the women who made the earthenware pots and basins for food and drink. The women also tended the crops alongside the men and, according to the memories of Olaudah Equiano, the women even marched with the men into battle and fought their enemies no less fiercely.

And the women, of course, did the cooking. It was not a very complicated task, as eighteenth-century Ibo cookery was extremely simple. They stewed their meat – mostly beef, goat or chicken – in big pots, and flavoured it with coarse pepper and a kind of salt made from wood ash. Their main vegetables were beans, yams (a starchy root), maize (sweet corn), and plantains (a type of banana). Palm trees, besides giving oil and nuts, provided palm wine – the sap of the tree, which was tapped and collected in gourds. Olaudah Equiano says he never saw anyone drunk on palm wine in his village, but if that were so his people must have had very strong heads, for palm wine is powerful stuff.

The 'house' of a village chief like Olaudah's father was not a house as we think of it, but something more like an estate, consisting of many buildings inside a boundary wall made of the hard red earth of the country. The individual buildings were little one-storey thatched houses, most having only one room and some having one side open. The biggest of them, standing in the centre of the compound, was the master's. It had two rooms, one for him to sit in with his family, and one for entertaining guests. His sleeping quarters were in another building, and he shared them with his sons. The walls of this dormitory were plastered with a mixture containing cow dung, which kept out unpleasant insects. Nearby buildings contained living and sleeping quarters for the chief's wives: a man was allowed more than one wife, although a woman could have only one husband. The other houses, farthest from the centre, were for slaves and their families.

Although these people had slaves, slavery in Africa was nothing like slavery in the plantations of America and the West Indies. Slaves were usually treated like junior members of the family – a rank below the master's wives, just as the wives were a rank below the master.

Though he had no formal lessons, young Olaudah was taught

'An End to Happiness'

all he needed to know, which was mainly how to hunt with a spear and how to fight. From an early age the Ibo children worked with their parents in the fields. There was education, although no school, and in the same way there was religion, although no church.

Ibo religious beliefs were not much like the Christian religion. They were more like the religion of the ancient Romans, who believed that everything – objects like doors and boundary stones as well as living creatures – had a 'spirit'. Like the Romans, the Ibo sacrificed animals to their supreme god, who was a rather vague kind of god connected with the sun. Again like the Romans, they believed in omens, good and bad, and they felt that the spirits of their dead ancestors were always near them. Olaudah as a small boy sometimes went with his mother to make offerings at his grandmother's tomb. His mother would spend most of the night there, groaning and lamenting. The tomb was in a lonely place, and poor little Olaudah was often frightened stiff, crouching in the dark listening to his mother's moans.

On market days Olaudah walked with his mother to the market, where the villagers sold salt and sweet-smelling woods in exchange for guns, hats, beads and dried fish (a great luxury as there were no large rivers or lakes in their neighbourhood). The men who sold them these goods came from somewhere farther south. They were powerful, silent, mahogany-coloured men, who sometimes bought slaves in the market. Olaudah's people would sell criminals or prisoners of war to passing slave-traders, though not their own house slaves.

The fact that the slave trade existed made life more dangerous and more violent. The slave-traders would come to a chief and ask if he would sell them slaves. They would offer a tempting price – French-made muskets, perhaps, or sparkling glass beads. Probably the chief had no slaves to sell, but he knew, or the slave-traders suggested to him, how he might get some. His people were almost sure to be on bad terms with some neighbours, and an excuse could easily be found to attack them, though the real purpose was to capture people to sell to the slave-traders.

The Savage Trade

There was another, even nastier way for the traders to get slaves – by kidnapping. The young Olaudah noticed the large sacks carried by the mahogany men he saw at the market, and wondered what they were for. Sadly for him and his family, he was to find out all too soon.

Sometimes, when the children of the village were not wanted in the fields, they were left behind to play in one of the village compounds. One or two of them would climb into the trees to act as look-outs in case of enemies. Olaudah, then aged ten or eleven, was acting as sentry one day when from his position high in the tree he saw a strange man slinking into a yard where there were several children. He shouted an alarm and the bigger children, flinging ropes around the intruder, managed to capture him.

Not long after that, Olaudah was left behind in his father's house with his sister, who was a year or so older, while the others were out working. Three people, two men and a woman, clambered silently over the wall and, before the children could cry out, they were seized, gagged and carried off into the woods. The event which, as Olaudah Equiano wrote thirty years later, 'put an end to all my happiness' was over in less than a minute.

All that day and the next their captors hurried through the forest, stopping for the night in a lonely hut which had probably been used by them many times before. On the second day they came near some travellers, and Olaudah started to shout for help. But the kidnappers quickly gagged him again and put him into a large sack.

On the third morning the two children were separated. Olaudah's sister was taken off by some new people. He never saw or heard of her again.

Olaudah himself was sold, and then sold again many times – each time for a higher price. Though he did not know it, he was moving steadily nearer the coast. One of his masters was a smith in a pleasant village, and in a different situation Olaudah might have enjoyed helping to make gold bracelets and anklets. But he could not forget his situation even for an hour. As a slave boy, he was not allowed to eat with the children of his master. For the son of a chief this was an extra shock on top of

'An End to Happiness'

the horror of being snatched away from home and family. One night he ran away, but he was many, many miles from his village and hardly knew which way to go towards it. Realizing that he could never find the way home, he crept back to his master's house, the only place he knew.

He was soon sold again, and this time found himself among people who spoke a different language. Unable to talk to his masters, to say he was hungry or tired or afraid, he came at last to the sea coast.

The first thing he saw was a slave ship riding at anchor, waiting to have her holds filled with slaves. He could hardly understand what the ship was, and had no word for it in his language. How did the thing move or stop? It seemed to be done by magic.

He had little time to wonder as he was carried on board and roughly manhandled by the sailors to see if he was a fit specimen to buy. Like the many thousands who had passed this way before, the little Ibo boy was almost paralysed with terror. Everything was so utterly strange and inexplicable. What was this great 'hollow place' that sat on the waters and moved with the wind? What were these waters that stretched without end, covering the whole world? Strangest of all, what were these hideous creatures who poked and pressed him? With their pale, sick-looking skins, like animals that live under a stone, and their horrible lank hair hanging loose from their heads like ropes, surely they were devils.

On the ship were many black people like himself, all looking miserable and frightened. Seeing a big copper pot on the deck, Olaudah was convinced that these evil spirits were going to cook him and eat him. So great was his terror that he fainted and fell on the deck. When he came to, some of the Africans tried to cheer him up, and a slave brought him a tot of rum. He was too frightened to drink it, but he did discover that there were people on board who spoke his language – one small comfort in his nightmare plight. They told him that he was not going to be eaten. These white men, they said, came from a far country. They wanted black men to work for them, and would carry them to their country.

The title page of Olaudah Equiano's autobiography, with a picture of the author. He was one of several Africans, former slaves, who lived in England in the eighteenth century.

For a time the eleven-year-old Olaudah felt a little better. Working was certainly preferable to being eaten. But it was hard to believe that nothing worse was in store for him. Looking at the white men and seeing the brutal cruelty with which they treated not only the blacks but other whites as well, he could not quell the fear that these savages would surely kill him.

'An End to Happiness'

An African Rebel

Most Africans who were sold as slaves to European dealers on the coast were half-paralysed with terror and unable to think of escaping, even if it were possible. But some did fight back against indignity and cruelty.

Slave-traders had no respect for individuals; they did not care if their slaves were humble peasants or princes of some African state, and it sometimes happened that a man of high position, accustomed to power and respect, was captured or kidnapped and sold to the slavers. A man like that, a proud leader of his own people, was not easily subdued. Now and then we hear of courageous resistance – a sudden flash of defiance from a brave and proud man like the man called 'Captain Tomba'.

In 1721, two English warships called at Sierra Leone. As Royal Navy vessels they were not, of course, engaged in the slave trade, but were looking for the famous pirate, Captain Roberts, who had recently raided several trading stations in West Africa. On board one of the ships was a surgeon named John Atkins, and it is through him that we hear of Captain Tomba. In the book he later wrote about the voyage, Atkins included the following account:

> The slaves when brought here [to the English trading station] have chains put on, three or four linked together under the care of their gromettoes [servants of the dealers] till opportunity of sale. They go at about £15 a good slave ...
>
> As these slaves are placed under lodges near the owner's house, for fresh air, cleanliness and customers better viewing them, I had every day the curiosity of observing their behaviour, which with most of them was very dejected. Once, on looking over some of old Cracker's slaves, I could not help taking notice of one fellow among the rest, of a tall, strong build, and bold, stern aspect. As he imagined we were viewing them with a design to buy, he seemed to disdain his fellow-slaves for their readiness to be examined, and as it were scorned looking at us, refusing to rise or stretch out his limbs as the master commanded, which got him an unmerciful whipping from Cracker's own hand with a cutting strap. He would certainly have killed him but for the loss he

himself would sustain. All of this the Negro bore with magnanimity, shrinking very little, and shedding a tear or two which he endeavoured to hide as though ashamed of. All the company grew curious at his courage, and wanted to know how Cracker came by him. He told us that this same fellow, called Captain Tomba, was a leader in some country villages that opposed them and their trade at the River Nunes, killing our friends there and firing their cottages. The sufferers, by the help of my men (says Cracker) surprised and bound him in the night about a month ago, though he killed two of them before they could secure him, and from thence he was brought hither and made my property . . .

Brutal treatment did not crush Captain Tomba. Soon afterwards, he was sold in a batch of thirty men and women to Captain Harding of the *Robert*, a Bristol ship. While the *Robert* was still lying moored offshore, Tomba planned an escape. He persuaded one of the women, who were less strictly guarded than the men, to help him. Three or four men agreed to take a chance as well. One night the woman came to him to say there were only five sailors on deck and all of them asleep. She also brought a heavy hammer – the best weapon she could find. Tomba roused his companions, but now that the moment had come only one of them was brave enough to join him. The three of them climbed on to the deck where three sailors were snoring. Creeping up to the nearest, Tomba swung the hammer and struck him a terrific blow on the temple, killing him instantly. Leaping across the deck, he dealt with the second in the same way. The third was awakened by the noise, but before he could move, Tomba's fellow conspirators grabbed him fast. A third blow of the hammer ended his resistance.

By that time the two remaining members of the watch were awake and on their guard. The captain had also heard the commotion and came running on deck, grabbing an iron hand spike on the way, to find his men struggling with the escapers. It took several blows of the hand spike before Tomba fell unconscious to the deck. The plot had failed, and the three conspirators were hastily bound with chains.

All slaving captains went in fear of a revolt among their captives and made bloody examples of any who dared resist. Tomba and the other man were too valuable to be killed, so

'An End to Happiness'

Revolt of the slaves. Ships' captains were very nervous of a rebellion by their 'cargo', who far outnumbered the crew.

they were savagely flogged and chained up in the hold. Three others, weaker men and so less valuable, who had known about the plot but taken no part in it, were killed instead. One of them was forced to eat the heart and liver of his companion who had been killed first. The woman was tied up by her thumbs in sight of all, flogged, and slashed with knives until she died.

Olaudah Equiano was one of the lucky ones. In the West Indies he was bought by a Captain Pascal, who named him Gustavas Vasa, after a famous ruler of Sweden, and that was the name he was known by for the rest of his life. With Captain Pascal he travelled widely, and he was present at some of the naval battles of the Seven Years' War (1756–63). He was in England for a time, and several people were kind to him, helping him to learn English and then sending him to school. Later he was owned by an American merchant, for whom he worked as a shipping clerk. This man was a member of the Christian sect called Quakers, and the Quakers were against slavery. Although he was reluctant to let so good a servant go, in 1766 Equiano's master allowed him to buy his freedom for £40. That was a large sum in those days; someone must have lent him the money. Ten years had passed since Equiano had been kidnapped into slavery, yet he was still only about twenty-one when he became a free subject of the king of England.

For the rest of his life, Olaudah Equiano, or Gustavas Vasa, lived mainly in England. He worked for the campaign against the slave trade, and he tried to get back to Africa as a missionary or explorer. But he never made it. He married an Englishwoman, but had no children so far as we know. He wrote his autobiography, first published in 1789 (a shorter edition with an introduction by Paul Edwards was published by Heinemann in London in 1967). Olaudah Equiano died in 1797, in his early fifties, and was soon forgotten.

John Atkins's book, in which he relates the failure of Captain Tomba's attempt to escape from the slave ship, was called A Voyage to Guinea ... in His Majesty's Ships, the Swallow and Weymouth, and was published in 1735. He tells us no more of Captain Tomba, leaving him chained hand and foot in the slave ship.

'Old Cracker' was a disreputable 'independent trader' (in business on his own, not on behalf of the Royal African Company) at Sierra Leone. His real name was John Leadstine.

7

MEAN COASTS AND ROTTING CASTLES

WHEN trade began between Europe and Africa, the Europeans built castles and forts at places on the West African coast to protect their trade. The first and most famous was the Castle of Elmina ('the Mine'), begun by the Portuguese in 1482 and later captured by the Dutch. At one time or another, nine European nations had trade forts in West Africa, clustered most thickly on the Gold Coast (in modern Ghana).

The largest castles, like El Mina under the Dutch, or the English headquarters at Cape Coast Castle, were built of stone or brick, sometimes imported from Europe; but the smaller forts were often built of mud, like African houses. Oyster shells, broken up and burned on the beach, provided a rough kind of mortar. The purpose of these buildings was to defend the trade of the country against hostile Africans and against other Europeans, and to provide a base from which trade might expand. They contained living quarters for soldiers and officials, store-rooms for trade goods and for provisions, workshops specializing in ship repair, offices, and pens or dungeons for slaves: at Cape Coast Castle there was room for 1,000 slaves in an underground prison cut out of solid rock.

The trade forts were usually run by a business company, like the English Royal African Company in the early eighteenth century, which, in theory anyway, had total control of the trade. Independent traders, called 'interlopers', had to pay a tax of ten per cent to the Royal African Company, but they still made better profits because they had none of the expense of maintaining trading stations and forts. Governments were sometimes willing to support companies like the Royal African Company with special grants. But that was not enough. The Royal African Company was always in trouble, never made much profit, and had to be wound up in 1750, when a new company was created to take over its responsibilities. Permanent trade forts made life easier for the Company's ships. Instead of cruising up and down the coast buying a few slaves here and a few there, a process which could take many months, a ship might take on her full quota from the slaves held by a trading station and be gone from the unhealthy coast in a couple of days.

The European forts were built only with the permission of the local ruler and paid rent for the land they occupied. Africans were not always eager to have them, however. When the Portuguese asked Kwame Ansa for leave to build the Castle of El Mina, the King hesitated. He was aware, he said tactfully, of the high honour done him by this request. But such grand people as the Portuguese would not, he feared, be happy on the Gold Coast. Until this time he had noticed that the Portuguese traders in his country always seemed eager to finish their business and depart as quickly as possible. Now they talked of settling in the land. But the climate would surely be too harsh for them. It would be better to leave things as they were.

The Portuguese, however, were persuasive, and as the land they wanted was a rocky peninsula of no great value, Kwame Ansa eventually agreed to lease it to them.

In later times, when they had seen the advantages of close contact with the Europeans – especially access to guns – African rulers were less reluctant. Some even asked the French, the Dutch or the English to build a base on their territory. African towns soon grew up around European forts, if they were not there already. Where the European establishment was a big one, as at Cape Coast Castle, the fort dominated the town, but at many of the smaller, scruffier forts, it was the townspeople who called the tune. The Europeans might be driven out if their behaviour failed to please. Even Cape Coast Castle was once captured by the local people in its early days, and in later times, when it was the strongest castle on the Guinea Coast, it was attacked more than once as a result of some local quarrel, though it was not captured again.

Mean Coasts and Rotting Castles

A modern photograph of the castle of El Mina, one of the earliest and most famous European trading forts in West Africa. The original fort was built by the Portuguese; it passed into Dutch ownership, and was finally bought by the British in 1872. Today it is used as a barracks by the Ghana police, and part is open to tourists.

A view of Cape Coast castle in the eighteenth century. It was the headquarters of the English Royal African Company, eight miles along the coast from El Mina. An impressive and impregnable building in its prime, it could hold a thousand slaves in its dungeons. 'The keeping of slaves thus underground', a Frenchman remarked, 'is a good security to the garrison against any insurrection.'

The presence of a European fort was not always an advantage to the Africans even in affairs of trade. It meant that they could deal only with whichever nation happened to own the fort. (At other places trade was open, and local African merchants with goods to sell could take their choice among the ships of half a dozen nations.) On the other hand, a fort gave protection to the local people. If their town was attacked, they could take shelter behind the walls of the fort. The forts also created more employment; local fishermen and farmers helped keep the fort supplied with food. Although minor quarrels were frequent, as a result of language difficulties or the confusing complications of the market place, as a rule the Europeans in the forts kept on good terms with the Africans outside. The Africans were often sorry when the whites left. Long after the French and the British had given up their trading posts at Whydah, the local people went on raising the French and British flags over the crumbling ruins.

As time went on the Africans became more 'Europeanized', picking up the customs of the whites in the fort, and bearing their children; there were no white women in West Africa. By the nineteenth century the populations of the little garrison towns were a mixture of races, almost as European as African.

The number of men in the European forts was never very large. The factor at Fort Commenda had only three or four soldiers and his second-in-command under him, and that was not the smallest of the Royal African Company's trading posts. At El Mina in the mid-seventeenth century, soon after the Dutch had taken it over from the Portuguese, there were 84 whites as well as 184 African slaves who worked for the Dutch Company and were not for sale to slave ships. The English, who were short of men, had even smaller garrisons than the Dutch or the French. Their buildings were less strongly built than those of the Dutch, though no worse than those of the French, who generally built in mud, not stone.

Grand castles like Elmina were uncommon. Most forts were built badly in the first place and never properly maintained. The governor of Cape Coast Castle was quite used to messages like this from the man in charge at Fort Commenda: 'I am sorry to inform you that yesterday the interior part of the Cook Room gave way, and it was with great difficulty that the cook escaped being buried under the rubbish.' There was a Danish fort which had a level roof (on which several cannon stood), made of flat stones and plaster supported by the trunks of coconut palms. Unfortunately, the ends of the palm trunks rotted, and every three or four years the roof collapsed into the rooms below and had to be rebuilt.

Life in a European trade fort in the eighteenth century was not pleasant. It was boring and at the same time dangerous. Danger came not so much from war or violence as from disease, for nothing was known of tropical diseases like malaria, yellow fever or sleeping sickness. To be sent out to a Gold Coast fort for a three-year posting was to be given an even chance of life or death. The captain of a ship on one West Africa cruise thought it lucky that only ten members of his crew were dead by the time he reached home.

Yet life was also boring, because the inhabitants of the fort were stuck on their little bit of territory, forbidden to travel far from base, and had nothing to occupy their time except the usual daily tasks of cleaning weapons, shifting stores, giving orders, and so on. There was no entertainment apart from watching African dances and getting drunk. Frayed by heat, sickness and boredom as well as drink, tempers grew short. The accountant at Cape Coast Castle in 1780 vowed he would never again dine at the governor's table, he was so sick of the angry arguments that always broke out there, not to mention the tiresome boasts of the half-senile, half-sozzled old governor.

The best men were not to be found in West African trade forts. 'No one comes out here,' wrote a Dutch factor, Willem Bosman, at the end of the seventeenth century, 'who could live in Holland.' As for the English at Cape Coast Castle, they were such miserable wretches that the mere sight of them excited Bosman's pity. They wasted their strength in continual drinking and lusting after local women, with the result, Bosman believed, that they fell easy victims to disease. The Frenchman, Jean Barbot, who like Bosman was an intelligent man, superior to most European factors, wrote that the Europeans he met in West Africa were generally 'men of no education or principles, void of foresight, careless, prodigal, addicted to strong liquors', a desperate lot in fact.

The slave trade corrupted everyone connected with it – Africans and Europeans alike. The sordid existence of the men in the forts was itself a kind of slavery. And if life was boring and dangerous in a big place like Cape Coast Castle, then it was worse in smaller forts and in places where one or two independent traders eked out their wretched lives on the fringe of the hostile continent.

The Life of a Slave-dealer

Nicholas Owen was a European trader who lived on the Sherbro River, Sierra Leone, in the middle of the eighteenth century. He dealt in European goods bought from passing ships, and in African products such as ivory and camwood (used for dyeing cloth). But his main business was slaves.

Buying slaves, he used to complain, was a mighty troublesome business. In the first place, he had to dole out generous doses of strong liquor to the African traders before business began. Then he had to listen to noisy argument, complaints (when he refused to pay the price asked), and 'bad language' – though Owen, who had served on ships in his time, must have heard plenty of that before. Still, it was a far from honourable business. Both sides would cheat if they had the chance.

Owen knew that some people believed the slave trade was evil. But few merchants thought so, and his own conscience did not worry him. Slaves to him were just goods for sale. He had no more feeling for them than he had for a couple of elephant tusks or a load of red camwood.

Buying and selling in West Africa was amazingly complicated. For one adult male Owen would trade a whole list of goods which included guns and gunpowder, kettles and basins, knives, beads and silk handkerchiefs. Everything was valued in terms of 'bars'. Originally, these were bars of iron or lead which were a big item of trade in Africa, but the word had come to stand for a certain value, like a pound or a dollar. There were two kinds of bars, 'ship's bars' and 'country bars', and they had different values. But to say exactly what that difference was would be almost impossible, because a ship's bar might be worth more than a country bar if reckoned in guns, but less if reckoned in silk handkerchiefs! It seems remarkable that anyone could understand such a system. No wonder there were so many complaints of cheating.

Nicholas Owen's house on the River Sherbro. It had mud walls lined with matting and a thatched roof. Parts of the garden, in which he took such pride, are also visible.

Owen never made as much money as he hoped, and he resented paying taxes to the local kings, who demanded customs duties from all white traders. He had a poor opinion of these little rulers: drunken old men, he said scornfully, who had only a lace hat, a silver-headed cane and a mat to sit on to distinguish them from their subjects. However, if he wanted to carry on his business he had to pay taxes like everyone else.

Nicholas Owen, joined for a time by his brother Blayney, lived at first in the remains of an abandoned English fort on

York Island, seventeen miles (30 kilometres) from the mouth of the Sherbro River. The island was low and marshy. Not much grew there except palm trees, and it was said to be unhealthy for Europeans. But it had the great advantage of being close to the centre of trade, so it was usually occupied by one or two white traders, like the Owens, willing to risk their health for the sake of possible riches. The Owen brothers soon found their own health was suffering, and as trade was not as good as they had expected they decided to move to a quieter place, on the river bank farther south, where they lived under the protection of a local trader who was half-African and half-English and went by the name of Mr Tucker.

The house of a European trader in West Africa was not built to last long, but it could be built quickly. Its walls were of mud plastered on a framework of long sticks and then whitewashed. The roof was thatched and the earth floor covered with mats. Another flimsy building nearby housed three or four servants. Apart from them, Owen lived rather like a hermit, trading with European ships once or twice a month but otherwise seeing no one.

Sometimes he went trading in a small boat up the rivers. He would sleep on his boat, lying under the sky on a colourful West African mat and covered only by a cotton cloth. His food was simple. The main items were rice and chicken, sometimes salted fish, palm oil and a local sauce, rather peppery. European provisions like tea and coffee were rare luxuries.

Owen was often ill, and in the suffocating hot weather felt constantly feverish. His sleep was disturbed by mosquitoes, and once by the croaking of a great frog under his bed; chased out and killed, it was over eight inches long. In the brassy heat of the day the frogs were silent and the mosquitoes disappeared, but their place was taken by large flies which left aching swellings where they had bitten right through Owen's shirt.

Owen hated West Africa and everything about it. 'A man in this country', he wrote in his diary, 'can have but little pleasure of his life when he considers what it is to live in England, the happiness of conversation, the pleasures of a life free from all the inconveniences of the wilderness.' Although he was interested (but not very deeply) in African customs, he disliked and did not understand the local people. In his gloomy moods, depressed by fever, he swore they were barbarous savages, hardly better than animals. He had no respect for their laws or religion (surprising though it may be, Owen himself was a religious man). Except when it was necessary he had nothing to do with the people he lived among.

Like many another man who has gone out into the world to make a fortune, Owen dared not return home until he had succeeded. He felt chained to Africa as securely as the men he bought and sold were chained to the slave benches. Sadly he wrote that he had spent the best years of his life in dull obscurity, all pleasures absent, in his mud hut on the Sherbro River. Eight years had passed, he remembered, since he had visited England or received a letter from home.

His worst problem was boredom. Once his brother had moved away there was no one he could talk to, since he never learned the local language. He did not go out and about more than necessary because it was dangerous. His business hardly occupied his time either. Trade was very slow at this time (1756–9) because of a European war which sharply cut down the number of merchant ships visiting West Africa. Owen just did not have enough to do. At Christmas 1756 he wrote in his diary: 'Arrived at York Island. October, November and December have passed without anything remarkable.' Three months and nothing had happened worth noting in his diary! A dull life indeed, yet in one way Owen might consider it fortunate that he had nothing remarkable to record. When something remarkable *did* happen, it was usually something bad.

In happier moods, Owen admitted that life had a few small comforts. He was glad to be out of the bustle of the world and away from the strife of war in Europe. He took pleasure in his garden, where he grew watermelons, pumpkins, a type of bean and other things. He got his servants to build little walls to keep out land crabs and snakes, though unfortunately there was no way to keep out a swarm of locusts which swept through the country from the north, consuming all crops.

Owen was happier in his garden than anywhere else, and he

The Savage Trade

A drawing made by Nicholas Owen of 'dancing priests', watched by an elephant and a seated man, with African drums, who may be Owen himself.

disliked being interrupted when some canoes arrived full of noisy people with goods to sell. One had camwood, another chickens, a third bunches of bananas or some rice. One complained that he had not been given his tot of spirits, another that he had not had his present of tobacco, a third that he was hungry and required food. Owen sighed with relief when they were gone and he could return to planning a new patch where he hoped to plant mustard.

Animals aroused his curiosity now and then. A local king gave him a chameleon as a pet, but it escaped after a few days by biting through the string around its leg. Other animals were less welcome, especially the 'tyger' (probably a leopard) that passed by night, leaving large footprints in the sand, and the spider, killed in the cookroom, which had legs as thick as the stem of a tobacco pipe.

Owen had few amusements. He kept his diary, not every day, though he sometimes wrote several pages at a time. He drew sketches, and he made designs out of small seashells, an idea he picked up from a ship's captain – another man whose job left him with nothing much to do for long periods.

So the tedious hours passed. 'As for this place I have no comfort or affection for it or its inhabitants, otherwise than it helps my fortune and puts me in a way of living independent at home.' Owen at least had hope of 'living independent'. The slaves he bought and sold did not have that, yet in other ways the life of the slave-dealer was almost as grim as the life of the slave. Sometimes, as he struggled with the depression that is one of the after-effects of malaria, Owen was overcome by despair. He feared he would never achieve his ambition of 'living independent'. In his diary he wrote more and more how vile his life was and how he longed for Europe: 'We spend the prime of youth among negroes, scraping the world for money, the universal god of mankind, until death overtakes us.'

A few months after he wrote those words, death overtook Nicholas Owen. Malaria, yellow fever or another of the diseases of the coast finished him off at last as it finished so many like him. No pleasant little property on the Avon or the Liffey for Nicholas Owen; only death among the mosquitoes in a mud hut on the Sherbro.

Nothing is known of Nicholas Owen except what he wrote in his diary, not even for certain that his name was Nicholas (he wrote only a shortened form, 'Nics'). He was born in Ireland and left to seek his fortune at sea in about 1746. After eight years at sea he and his brother lost all their possessions when their ship was captured in West Africa, where, not having the means to go anywhere else, they settled in 1754. They worked for an English trader for a while and in 1756 became independent traders themselves. Three years later Nicholas was dead. His diary somehow found its way to England and was published by Routledge in 1930 (Journal of a Slave Dealer, *edited by Eveline Martin*).

8

FLOATING COFFINS

THE voyage that carried Africans into slavery across the Atlantic was called the 'Middle Passage'. It was the second and most important part of a three-lap voyage: the first lap was from Europe to West Africa, the second from West Africa to the West Indies or the Americas, and the third from America home to Europe. Because of the direction of winds and currents in the North Atlantic, it was easier for a sailing ship bound from West Africa to Europe to sail via the West Indies than to sail direct. From the shippers' point of view, therefore, this 'triangular trade' was highly convenient.

From Europe the ships carried European manufactures to West Africa, where they traded them for slaves. The slaves were sold in the West Indies or, less often, on the American mainland. After a thorough cleaning, the ships took on a cargo of sugar, rum, tobacco, coffee and other products of the colonial plantations for sale in Europe.

American ships also took part in the profitable slaving business, but their 'triangle' was a different shape. From ports like Boston and Newport, the American ships, which were smaller than the European slave ships, set out for the Guinea coast. They were often captained by men who were not professional sailors but tradesmen or farmers who had been offered the job because they were honest men and liked the idea of a challenging sea voyage. The Europeans called their ships 'rum boats', because rum was the cargo they usually carried. The Africans had come to like rum even more than French brandy. Having sold their rum in exchange for men in West Africa (or occasionally East Africa), the 'rum boats' made for the West Indies. It was easier to sell slaves in the islands than on the

Floating Coffins

mainland, and besides they could pick up a cargo of molasses, which they carried home to New England to be made into rum, completing the 'triangle'.

Someone cruising along the coast of Guinea in the eighteenth century would have seen, dotted along the coast, the ships of half a dozen nations waiting to be 'slaved'. In some places, like

The map shows the routes of the chief slave-trading nations in the eighteenth century. The Portuguese had been driven out of Guinea and supplied their plantations in Brazil with slaves from Angola. The West Indies were supplied by the British, the French and the Dutch, whose main trading centre was the island of Curaçao in the Dutch Antilles. Some slaves were shipped direct to the English colonies in North America, but more often they arrived via the West Indies.

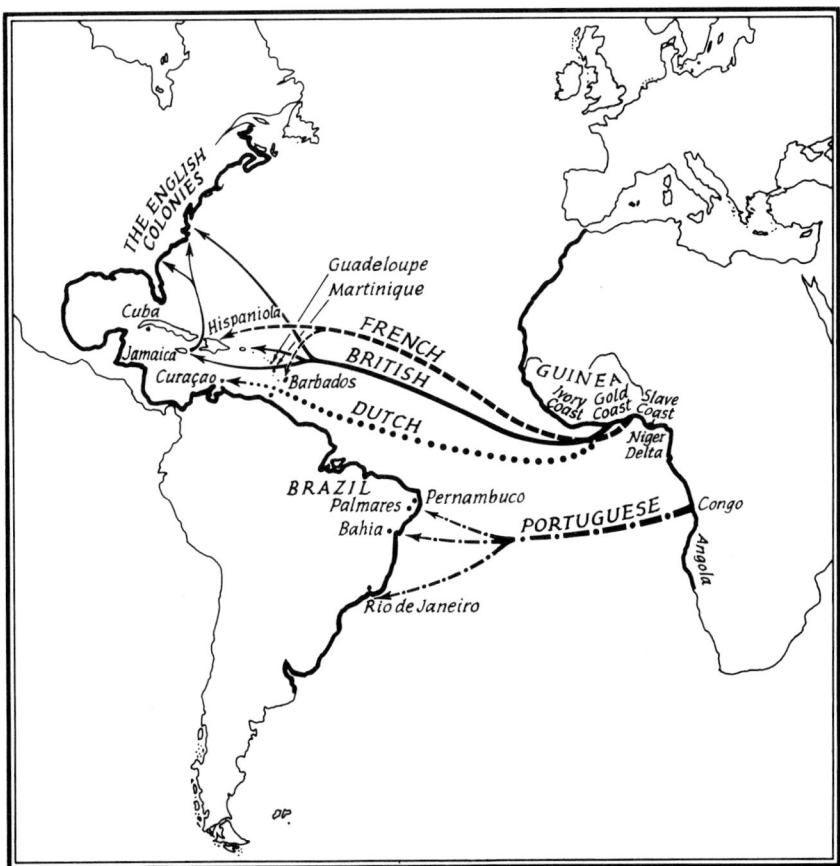

the Bonny River (Nigeria) there could be as many as ten ships waiting at the same time, for it often took several months for a large slave ship to fill her holds. It might be necessary to visit several places, buying one or two slaves at each. The delay was longest on the Gold Coast, where competition was greatest. In other parts, Portuguese Angola for example, a lucky captain could be away in a week or two.

Once the ship was moored and the sails furled, the crew set about turning her into a combined office and reception centre by making what they called a 'house'. The roof was made by tying a spar between the masts, with other spars, like the rafters of a roof, running from the horizontal 'beam' to the deck. Over this framework the sailors laid mats made of rushes. The 'house' was divided by a wooden partition, to make two compartments, one for the crew, where visiting kings and caboceers were entertained, the other for receiving the slaves. The roof did not keep out the rain very well, but it did keep out fresh air, making the 'house' hot and stuffy. The atmosphere was not improved by the smoke of open fires burning in braziers on the deck.

The period of waiting was the worst time for a ship in the triangular trade, and captains were anxious to make their stay as brief as possible. The crew was small, especially on ships owned by Liverpool merchants, who were keen to keep costs as low as possible, and it usually grew smaller as tropical diseases took their toll of the crew. There were not enough sailors to guard the slaves, and some captains appointed a few slaves to stand guard over the others, arming them with whips which, taking their example from the whites, they were not slow to use. All the same, there was an obvious danger in this system, especially if all the slaves on board belonged to the same nation. It was safer if those put in charge were strangers to the rest.

The slaves came aboard in dug-out canoes, which were often manned by Krumen, men from the Grain Coast whose traditional occupation, fishing, made them expert boat-handlers. The slaves were shackled in pairs with leg-irons. They were branded with a red-hot iron, like cattle, to show who owned

The Rev. John Newton (1725–1807), who worked on a slave ship and as a factor in West Africa as a young man. Years later he became a priest and a strong opponent of the slave trade. 'I think I should have quitted [the trade] sooner, had I considered it as I do now,' he wrote, 'to be unlawful and wrong. But I never had a scruple upon this head at the time; nor was such a thought once suggested to me by a friend.'

them; their heads were shaved and their clothes taken away. Before they were bought, they had to undergo a rough and brutal medical examination to make sure they were in good condition. Special attention was paid to the teeth, tell-tale evidence of age. Once on board the men were kept in chains until the ship sailed, and sometimes for the whole length of the Middle Passage. Women and children were allowed to go free. Young women and girls were at the mercy of crude, sex-starved sailors, and although sexual relations with the captives were forbidden on some ships, on many others rape was just one of the cruelties of the voyage.

The slaves were housed, like any other cargo, in the ship's hold. The hold was usually about five feet (1·6 metres) high, so a man could not stand up straight. However, the slaves were not expected to stand, and a way was found of cramming in even more captives by building a shelf, six feet (2 metres), wide around the sides of the ship; in larger ships there were two shelves. The slaves lay on the bottom of the hold and on the shelves, each with about twenty inches (0·5 metres) of vertical space. It was thus impossible even to sit upright, and as long as they were in the hold the slaves were forced to lie flat. Packed in, as one captain said, 'like books on a shelf', they could not lie on their backs, because a person on his back takes up more space than one lying on his side. As the men were still fettered in pairs, left leg of one to right leg of his partner, it was obviously more uncomfortable for them to lie on their sides. In fact, if the only purpose of the slave ships had been to make the existence of the slaves as hellish as possible, it is hard to imagine what more could have been done.

Slave ship captains were glad to get away from the African coast, away from the deadly fevers and the danger – always present while the ship lay close to shore – that the slaves would mutiny. But even after sailing the dangers were not over. The ships had neither the space nor the men to look after their captives, though their treatment might be better or worse according to the character of the captain himself. There were some captains who were, within limits, kind men, like John Newton who later became a parish priest and wrote several hymns still sung in English churches, or Hugh Crow, who always boasted that he was liked not only by his crew, which was unusual, but also by his slaves, which is hard to believe. There were also captains who were cruel, vicious and evil, who ruled their ships by terror and the whip. Captain McTaggart of the *Alexander* was one of those who, corrupted by the absolute power which the captain of a ship holds, delighted in cruelty. On one voyage he had every member of his fifty-man crew flogged except three. If anyone dared complain, he set his Newfoundland dog on him. One desperate sailor jumped overboard to escape a flogging. He was picked up and, when asked if he were not afraid of being eaten by sharks, answered, 'I preferred that to life on this ship.'

Once the ship was at sea, the slaves were brought up out of their steamy dungeon below decks each morning. The men's leg irons were linked to a chain running down the centre of the ship to prevent them jumping overboard. Though little was known of health or hygiene, the slavers dimly understood that fresh air and exercise were necessary. The slaves were therefore made to perform a gloomy dance on the deck, the whips of the crew encouraging them to show plenty of vigour. Some ships had a drummer or a piper who played while the captives danced. Being compelled to jump about while wearing heavy leg irons caused bruising and bleeding around the ankles, but only a few captains were prepared to take the fetters off.

On deck the slaves would receive their meal, which was usually a kind of porridge made from maize or millet. Coarse beans, the kind fed to horses, made a change if not an improvement, and occasionally there was a little salted meat. A second meal was provided in the afternoon. It was often exactly the same as the first.

While the slaves were out on deck, a good captain had the slave decks washed down with warm vinegar and scrubbed. Some did not bother, and if the weather was rough the slaves were never allowed out at all. The state of the hold then became unbearable – dark, stuffy and stinking. So foul was the smell of the slave ships that other vessels took care to steer to windward of them. Richard Drake, who spent many years'

The Savage Trade

The scene on a French slave ship in the early nineteenth century, with slaves forced to perform a miserable dance on the deck as exercise to keep them healthy.

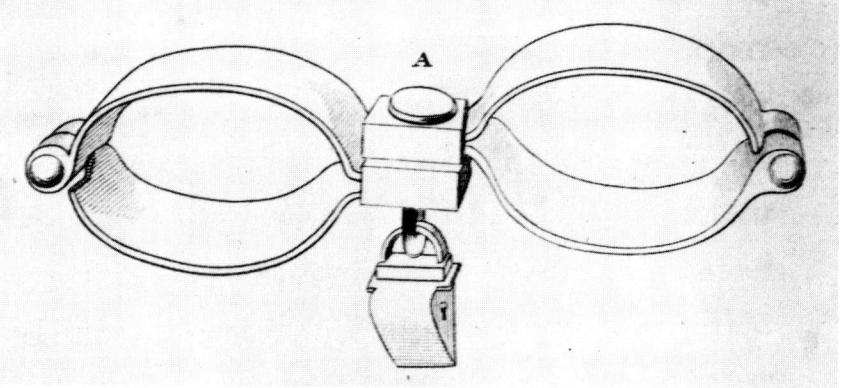

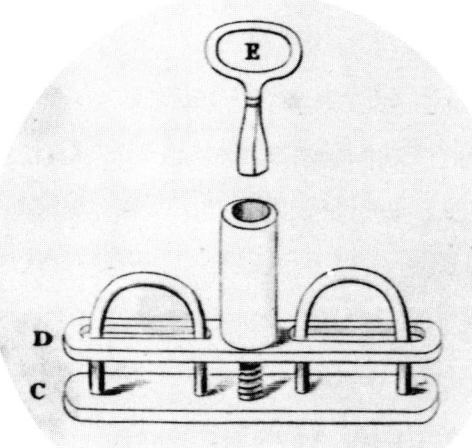

Handcuffs and a thumbscrew (left), which pressed the thumb until the blood burst through the skin. They were made and sold in Liverpool in the eighteenth century for use in slave ships.

Floating Coffins

A branding iron, which was used to burn the owner's initials (GHC) into the flesh of a slave – the chest of a man, the shoulder of a woman.

service in slave ships, used to go around holding a bag containing strong-scented camphor in his teeth.

Alexander Falconbridge, who was ship's surgeon on several slave ships and later wrote a book about his experiences, left a grim record of conditions on the slave deck. Each man had less room than he would have had in his coffin, and as there was no spare space it was impossible to move about without stepping on human bodies. With tarpaulins over the gratings and air vents to keep out the rain and spray, it was almost pitch dark and hard to see where you were treading. The surgeon used to take off his shoes to avoid injuring the people he was forced to scramble over. Some of them used to bite his feet when he stepped near their faces. The slaves themselves had to move about in order to reach the lavatories – two or three large buckets for perhaps a hundred men – and each man had to take with him the partner to whom he was chained. In fact, the journey to the buckets was so difficult that many just gave up the effort to reach them. As the captives often suffered from dysentery, an infectious (and often fatal) disease like an acute form of diarrhoea, the state of their prison became more foul than can be easily described. With ventilation blocked off, the heat was so great that many fainted. Falconbridge could only compare the conditions of such a place with those of a slaughter-house. Epidemics raged through the holds, with smallpox especially deadly among the Africans. Apart from disease, many died from no evident cause, a few went mad, and others managed to kill themselves. One man on the *Brookes* tried to cut his throat the first night out. Dr Trotter sewed up the wound, but the next night, with no other weapon than his finger nails, the man tore out the stitches. Again the surgeon patched him up, and this time his hands were tied behind his back. He then refused to eat, despite threats and punishment, and in a week or two he was dead.

Some of the Africans believed that if they died they would return to their homeland, and that made suicide less frightening. One captain, after losing some who had jumped overboard and, with expressions of joy on their faces, disappeared beneath

Below decks on a slave ship. This is a sketch in watercolours by a young English naval officer who was present when this ship was captured – after the slave trade had been made illegal.

the ocean, swore that if anyone else tried to do the same he would fish out his body and cut off his head. Then, he said, if he went home he would have to go headless. Those who refused to eat were flogged until they did, and if that did not work a special instrument was used which forced the jaws open so that food could be pushed into their mouths.

Yet some still died from no apparent cause except pure misery. European slavers called it 'fixed melancholy', and noticed that although slaves might recover from dysentery, smallpox, or any of the other African and European diseases that wafted through the slave-ships, none recovered from the 'fixed melancholy'. The sailors were puzzled, and some, seeing no other cause of death, believed that Africans were capable of holding their breath until they suffocated (which is, of course, impossible).

Conditions were not always as bad as those recorded by Alexander Falconbridge. Although the Africans were never treated as human beings, they were valuable cargo, and it was the captain's job to transport them to the West Indies alive and, if possible, in good health. It should also be remembered that conditions were almost as bad for the sailors as for the slaves. In fact, the proportion of sailors who died on the Middle Passage was slightly larger than the proportion of Africans. Unlike the Africans, they were not valuable. They were also in greater danger from certain diseases. Scurvy, for example, a disease caused by the lack of fresh food, was more common among the crews than on the slave decks, because the sailors were longer at sea.

A good captain like Hugh Crow managed several voyages without losing a single slave or sailor. But that was exceptional. It was not rare for hundreds to die in an epidemic; occasionally every African on board was dead by the time the ship entered Caribbean waters. In twenty voyages recorded by Thomas Clarkson, one of the chief opponents of the slave trade, a total of 7,904 slaves were embarked and 2,053 died, slightly over a quarter. The average loss was less than that, probably about one in eight.

The voyage from the Gambia to Barbados could take as little

An engraving from a daguerreotype (an early form of photograph) of the slave deck on the ship Wildfire, *brought into Florida after capture in 1860. Conditions on slave ships were, if possible, even worse after the slave trade had been banned. In the days when it was still legal there were at least some regulations, though often disobeyed, which governed the conditions in which slaves might be transported.*

as six weeks, but from, for example, Angola to Cuba it could last as long as three months, especially if the ship were becalmed in the doldrums. The longer the voyage, the greater the risks. Food ran low and so did water, and even if there were

Floating Coffins

TO BE SOLD & LET
BY PUBLIC AUCTION,
On MONDAY the 18th of MAY, 1829,
UNDER THE TREES.

FOR SALE,
THE THREE FOLLOWING
SLAVES,
VIZ.

HANNIBAL, about 30 Years old, an excellent House Servant, of Good Character.
WILLIAM, about 35 Years old, a Labourer.
NANCY, an excellent House Servant and Nurse.

The MEN belonging to "LEECH'S" Estate, and the WOMAN to Mrs. D. SMIT

TO BE LET,
On the usual conditions of the Hirer finding them in Food, Clothing and Medical Assistance.

THE FOLLOWING
MALE and FEMALE
SLAVES,
OF GOOD CHARACTERS,

ROBERT BAGLEY, about 20 Years old, a good House Servant.
WILLIAM BAGLEY, about 18 Years old, a Labourer.
JOHN ARMS, about 18 Years old.
JACK ANTONIA, about 40 Years old, a Labourer.
PHILIP, an Excellent Fisherman.
HARRY, about 27 Years old, a good House Servant.
LUCY, a Young Woman of good Character, used to House Work and the Nursery.
ELIZA, an Excellent Washerwoman.
CLARA, an Excellent Washerwoman.
FANNY, about 14 Years old, House Servant.
SARAH, about 14 Years old, House Servant.

Also for Sale, at Eleven o'Clock,
Fine Rice, Gram, Paddy, Books, Muslins, Needles, Pins, Ribbons &c. &c.

AT ONE O'CLOCK, THAT CELEBRATED ENGLISH HORSE
BLUCHER,

ADDISON PRINTER GOVERNMENT

A poster advertising a sale of slaves in the United States in the early nineteenth century.

plenty of both, the condition of the Africans in their beastly hold grew worse with every day at sea. There were other dangers that menaced any sailing ship: storm and shipwreck, piracy and warfare. During the eighteenth century Britain and France were at war almost as often as they were at peace, and slave ships, which were well-armed, had to be prepared to fight off attackers. Captain Crow seldom completed a triangular voyage without a fight. Once, when he was captain of the *Will* of Liverpool, he was attacked three times, first by a privateer (a ship licensed by the government to attack all enemy shipping in time of war), then by three frigates as he was lying in the Bonny River, and finally by an eighteen-gun warship. Thanks to his powerful ship's guns, some manned by the slaves he was carrying, he beat them all off.

On the better-run slave ships, the last few days of the voyage to the West Indies brought a short interval of relief. With the end of the voyage in sight, discipline was relaxed. Sometimes there was even a kind of party – a grim idea in view of the fate of most of the people on board – when African women dressed up in the clothes of the sailors and capered about on the deck.

Then came the final destination, and the sale of the 'cargo'. The usual method was by auction, when the Africans had to undergo again the ordeal of being inspected for physical faults as though they were carcases in a wholesale meat market. Even worse was the 'scramble', when the prospective buyers were let loose among the slaves and rushed about trying to seize those they wanted before anyone else did, like rats fighting over scraps of food. On top of all the suffering and indignity of the previous months, this terrifying ordeal was the last shattering blow.

Then the whole business was over. The captains totted up the profits, the crew began cleaning out the ship to take on a cargo of colonial produce (which had to be carried in better conditions than the slaves), and the Africans disappeared to the plantations and a life of perpetual slavery.

Floating Coffins

The Brookes

The *Brookes* was a Liverpool vessel of 320 tons, a typical slave ship of the late eighteenth century. She was licensed by the government to carry 454 slaves, each man being allotted a space measuring about six feet (2 metres) by eighteen inches (0·4 metres), less for women and children. In the plan, which was made by a captain in the Royal Navy in 1788, little figures are drawn to represent each slave. There are actually 451 figures, and the captain said he could not see how the remaining three were fitted in. But in the days before the law was passed which limited the number each ship could carry, the *Brookes* had often carried far more. According to the evidence of Dr Thomas Trotter, who sailed in her as ship's surgeon on more than one occasion, she had sometimes carried at least 600 slaves.

Mutiny

The Africans on a slave-ship far outnumbered the crew, even when all the sailors were fit, and in spite of the strict confinement and savage discipline on most ships, the possibility of mutiny by the prisoners was something that all captains feared.

In November 1749 the *Ann* of Liverpool, a small ship with a crew of thirteen, arrived off the coast of Guinea to trade for slaves. Six months later she was still there. She had about sixty Africans on board, but they were not carefully watched because most of the crew of the *Ann* were sick.

In the middle of the night the Africans turned on the crew. They had managed to get hold of guns and ammunition somewhere, and made short work of the sickly sailors, killing or wounding all but two who managed to hide. Taking over the ship, they ran her hard on shore, where she was soon broken up. The Africans plunged through the surf and disappeared into the trees.

'This,' said a Boston newspaper which reported the incident,

The Savage Trade

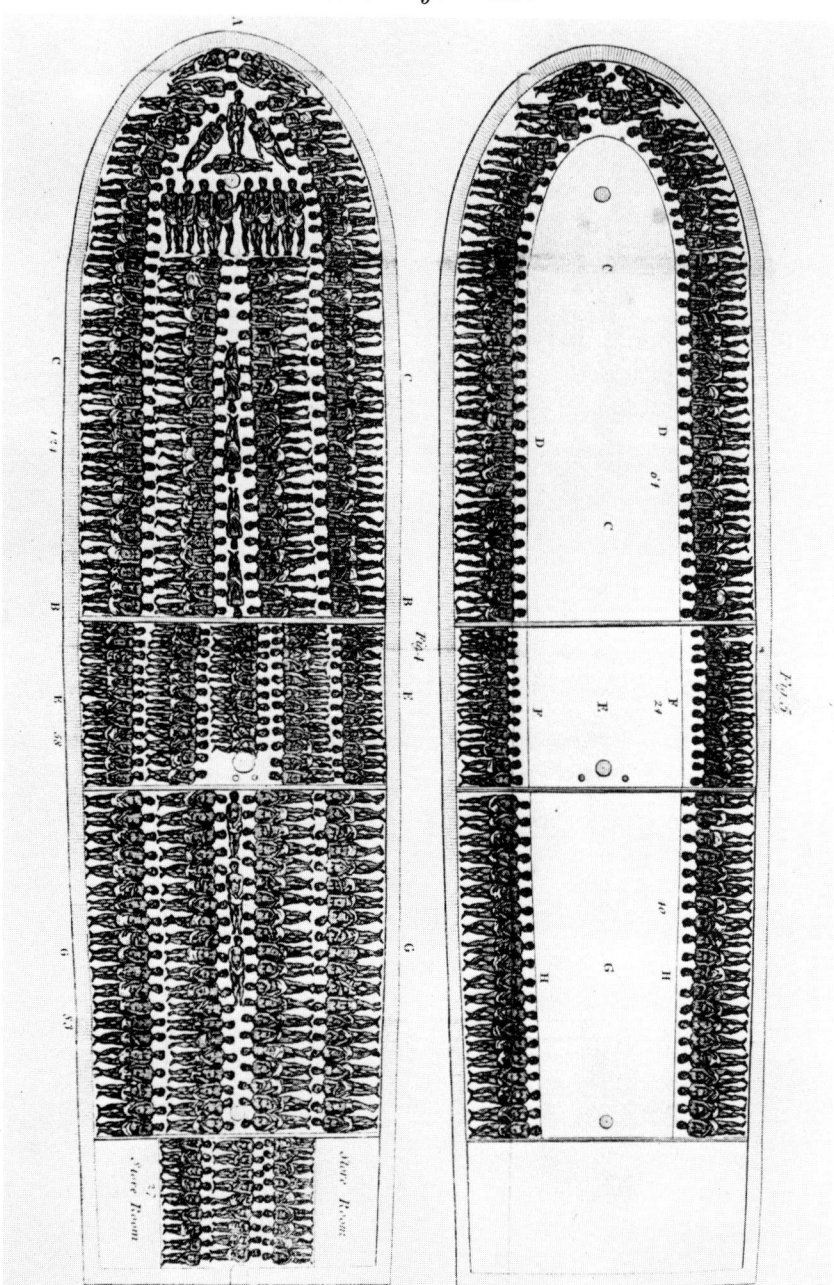

This notorious plan shows how the slaves were accommodated in the Liverpool ship Brookes, *with men towards the bow, boys in the centre, and women aft. The plan was used by Clarkson as part of the evidence he presented in his crusade against the slave trade (see Chapter 10).*

Floating Coffins

'should be a Caution of great Care and Vigilance to be used at that trade.' But, only four weeks later came news of another case in which 'great Care and Vigilance' had not been used.

The *King David* of Bristol left the Guinea coast in May 1750 with a cargo of slaves. Several members of her crew had died since leaving England, so she, like the Liverpool *Ann*, was undermanned. Her captain was an easy-going fellow, and the Africans on the ship were not kept in irons. One of them, a chief of some kind in his own country, spoke English well and was sometimes allowed into the captain's cabin for a talk. He did not fail to notice that weapons were kept in the captain's cabin.

This African chief (we do not know his name) was the leader of a group of fifteen who, soon after the ship sailed, rushed the cabin and seized the guns. The captain and five others were killed at once. The rest of the crew shut themselves into the hold for safety, but came out later when the African chief shouted down to them that they would not be killed if they came out peacefully. One man, the first mate, was suspicious of this promise and refused to come up. A boy was sent down to tell him that if he did not surrender he would be cut to pieces so, unwillingly, he left the hold. On deck he was quickly put in irons like the others who had surrendered earlier.

That evening at about eight o'clock the doubts of the first mate proved to be justified. Nine white sailors were thrown over the side by the Africans who now commanded the ship. As they were still in irons, they went down quickly.

The mate was about to be thrown over as well when the leader of the Africans stepped in. 'If you throw him into the sea,' he said, 'who will run the ship?' He swore he would kill the man who killed the mate. Reluctantly, they let him go.

Meanwhile, the ship drifted with the wind and tide, but these Africans or at least their leaders, knew more about the world than the people, often from deep in the interior of the continent, who usually made up the cargo of a slave ship. Some said they should make for Calabar, some for the little Portuguese island of São Thomé, but the chief told them that the safest course was to make for a place where there were no white men. He recommended a little island called Desiada which, he believed, Europeans never visited. The rest agreed.

The ship reached the island on 14 May, but what happened after that is a mystery. A boat was put out but it seems that it did not return, so the ship did not stop at Desiada after all. Eventually she reached another island, where she fell into the hands of the French. Those who survived of the crew were released, but what happened to the Africans is not recorded.

The Case of the Zong

The conditions of the Middle Passage were so bad that many Africans died on the voyage. However, the sole purpose of the voyage was to sell the Africans in the West Indies, and on every man, woman or child who died the slave-traders made a loss. Therefore they wanted the Africans to stay alive. They did not care about them as people; they *did* care about them as valuable cargo. If they could have sold dead bodies for the same amount as living people, no African would have been breathing when he or she reached the West Indies. Only their value as slaves kept them alive.

But a situation could arise in which the slaves were more valuable dead. In that case, the captain was tempted to commit mass murder. The worse case of this kind on record (there were probably others that nobody heard about) took place in 1781 on a British ship named the *Zong*.

The *Zong* left the Guinea coast on 6 September, bound for Jamaica. She had 440 Africans on board, and 17 whites. There was sickness on the ship, and by the time she reached the Caribbean some 60 Africans and 7 Europeans were dead. Many others were ill and unlikely to recover. On 27 November the ship came in sight of Jamaica but drew away again. Her captain, Luke Collingwood, said later that he mistook the island for another, but it is more than possible that his 'mistake' was deliberate.

On 29 November Collingwood called his officers together and proposed to them a grisly plan – to throw overboard all the Africans who were sick and, in his opinion, unlikely to recover. This, he said, would be no worse than allowing them to linger on a few more days in pain until they died anyway. He put

Slaves thrown overboard. In the case of the Zong, 122 people were drowned in an effort to claim the insurance, which would not have been payable if they had died on board. Such incidents were probably more common than we know; captains naturally kept quiet about them.

forward two more practical reasons. Water, he said, was running out, and it was necessary to sacrifice some lives in order to save others. The second reason was a little more complicated. Any slaves who died of natural causes on board ship represented a simple loss to their owners. But if they were thrown alive into the sea, then the owners would be able to claim insurance. Insurers would pay up for cargo which was thrown overboard in order to save the rest. Of course, the rule was meant to apply to ordinary trade goods, not human beings. Insurers refused to insure against death by natural causes, such as disease, because they feared that captains would be tempted to let all their slaves die in order to collect the insurance.

When Captain Collingwood explained his evil plan, only one officer protested. The mate, whose name was James Kelsal, objected that there was no shortage of water which would justify such an act. There is little doubt that he was right. Although the stock of water was certainly low, the men were still on full rations, and before the situation became really serious the stock was increased by rainfall. Captain Collingwood knew he was near land anyway. He cannot have been seriously worried by lack of water. His true motive was to claim the insurance.

The mate, after making his protest, said no more. He was one of those who, the same evening, threw 54 living people into the sea. Three days later (the day the rain fell) 42 more were cast overboard. A week afterwards, when the ship was a few miles from land, a third group of 26 were drowned. Their hands were tied together before they were thrown into the sea, and some of them, seeing this, jumped into the sea while they at least had the freedom to use their arms. But they too were drowned. A few days later the *Zong* anchored at Kingston, Jamaica, where the remaining Africans were sold.

The case of the *Zong* came to light when the insurers refused to pay for the drowned slaves and were sued by the owners. The owners won the case when the jury decided that throwing slaves overboard was no different, in law, from throwing horses overboard. The insurers appealed, and the verdict was reversed in another court, where Lord Mansfield decided that human beings, slaves or not, could not be treated as simple trade goods. By this time (1783) the crusade for abolition of the slave trade was going strong, and one of its leaders, Granville Sharp, took up the *Zong* case as an example of the hideous cruelties of slave-trading. This account is based on his report.

Captain Collingwood had died in the meantime, and although there was some talk of charging his officers with murder, nothing came of it.

Captain Hugh Crow, last of the Liverpool slaving captains, who convinced himself that the slave trade was a good thing for all concerned.

Captain Crow

Captain Hugh Crow was one of the last of the Liverpool slaving captains. He was born in the Isle of Man in 1765. As a child, out walking with his mother near the seashore, he saw the Liverpool ships passing and declared, 'Mother, I shall one day be captain of a ship like that.' Despite losing an eye in a childhood accident, he went to sea at seventeen as a ship's carpenter and eventually rose to achieve his ambition of commanding a Guinea ship.

Captain Crow had a high reputation with the Liverpool shipowners and with the marine insurers, as he had a better record than most for transporting slaves without loss. The grateful insurers once presented him with a silver plate worth £200 after he had fought off a French privateer and brought his cargo safely to market.

In his fashion, Crow looked after both crew and slaves well. He made sure that they had a proper diet, issued lime juice against scurvy, and gave them limewood sticks to chew to keep mouth and teeth healthy. He was on very good terms with the kings of Bonny (his usual West African port of call), who were as strong in support of the slave trade as Crow himself. They had many a drunken party, though Crow would become angry when King Pepple, tottering around the ship in scarlet boots several sizes too small, made fun of his beloved homeland, the Isle of Man, and he once chased him off his ship when Pepple remarked that the Isle of Man was such a miserably poor place it could not afford a king of its own. 'Poor boy,' roared Pepple, waving the rum bottle as his canoe was paddled away, 'you can't havee king!'

Captain Crow was proud of his popularity with blacks as well as whites. When he landed at Kingston, Jamaica, he often found a number of his 'old shipmates', as he called them waiting on the wharf to greet him. Some shook him by the hand, others called out greetings. Once, a group of them insisted on entering his cabin to welcome him. It was a Sunday morning, about 9 a.m., and Crow was still in his bunk when the mate came in to say that a great number of black men and women had come on board, all dressed in their best, and were anxious to see him. 'By all means,' he said, hastily throwing on his clothes, and in a moment they all rushed into the cabin, crowding around him and saying, 'God bless massa! How poor massa do?' They asked what fights he had had on the voyage, for Crow seldom completed a voyage without a tussle with a Frenchman.

Floating Coffins

Not only Frenchmen either. In 1806 he was in command of the *Mary*, bound for the West Indies, when two warships were sighted. As he was near French territory, he had little doubt they were French cruisers and, clapping on sail, tried to outrun them. As night approached, one of the strangers came up behind the *Mary* and ordered her to heave to. The order was given in English, but as that was a common ruse of French ships Crow paid no attention. Two shots were fired, and the *Mary* replied. The second ship then came up, and again shouts were heard across the water, but with the noise of wind and waves it was difficult to make out whether the accent was French or English. Both ships then engaged the *Mary*, and Crow fired back, not a bit dispirited, he said, although he admitted that he had got himself into 'a warm berth'. He was hit in the arm by a splinter, but in the darkness and confusion the crew did not see he had been wounded. Cannon balls were whistling about in such numbers that even the crash of a ball piercing the hull was hardly noticed. A shot that came through an open gun port cut off the boatswain's legs, and another burst into the hold, killing several Africans. For six hours the unequal battle continued, and the *Mary*'s ammunition was running low. Crow was hit again and fell to the deck, knocked out for a moment. The crew, feeling this was the end, gathered around him, and the chief mate struck the colours. As he got his breath back, Crow urged them to hoist the colours again and fire a final broadside, but he was finally convinced that he would have to surrender.

As the *Mary* heaved to, her sails and rigging in tatters and her hull leaking in several places, the attackers put out boats, and the crew began to gather their belongings, preparing to be taken off as prisoners of war. The boats came alongside, but when their occupants climbed on board they spoke in the accents of London, Sussex and Devonshire. The *Mary* had been engaged with two British men-of-war. When he heard this, Crow struck his head in rage against the cabin floor with such violence that his nose began to bleed. He afterwards swore that he never fully recovered from the injury he did himself in that moment of frustration.

The Savage Trade

Floating Coffins

The Mary, *commanded by Captain Crow, attacked by two British warships that took her for a French ship, 1 December 1806.*

The Savage Trade

The year after Crow's battle with his own countrymen, the slave trade was made illegal. The last (legal) slave ship to sail from Liverpool was commanded by Captain Crow, and when he returned he retired from the sea and settled in the Isle of Man. To the end of his days – he lived another twenty years – he remained convinced that the slave trade was an excellent thing for the British Empire, for his friends the slavery kings of Bonny, and for the Africans too, as the slaves he had met in Kingston, Jamaica, were, he insisted, much better off than they had been as free men in Africa. All Crow knew of Africa was the cruel and sordid slave-trade kingdoms of the coast, and all he knew of colonial slavery was what he saw in the streets of Kingston. Even he might have changed his opinion if he had seen the more peaceful villages of the African interior, or if he had witnessed the harsh life of the slaves on the plantations.

Captain Crow's *Memoirs* were published in 1830, not long after his death.

9

THE MERCHANTS

THE first slave-traders in Africa were the Portuguese. In the seventeenth century others, especially the French, the English and the Dutch, moved into the business. For a time the Dutch were the most efficient; they took over most of the Portuguese bases in Guinea. The Portuguese treated the Africans little better than others did, but at least regarded them as human beings. They insisted, for example, on baptizing all slaves before the Atlantic voyage, something the English thought laughable. After the Portuguese had been driven out of their strongholds in Guinea, they continued to ship slaves in large numbers from Angola.

Early eighteenth-century houses of rich merchants in Bristol.

The Savage Trade

The Merchants

During the eighteenth century Britain became the chief slave-trading nation. To begin with the London merchants of the Royal African Company controlled the trade, but independent traders were always more successful than the Company, and the port of Bristol soon replaced London as the chief slaving centre. Bristol was the second largest city in England, and its position on the west coast gave it an advantage over London in Atlantic trade. It was from Bristol, after all, that the earliest English voyages to America set out.

By about 1730, the year in which an Act of Parliament gave anyone the freedom to trade in slaves on payment of a small fee (£2), Bristol was being challenged by Liverpool, in the

The old Exchange building in Liverpool, decorated with African heads in plaster. All such symbols of Liverpool's once-proud association with the slave trade have been carefully removed.

A view of the port of Liverpool from the south-east, about 1770.

north-west. A small, struggling port in the seventeenth century, by 1725 Liverpool had grown into 'one of the wonders of Britain', according to Daniel Defoe. It was 'so great, so populous and so rich that it may be called the Bristol of this part of England'. It continued to grow throughout the century, thanks to the profits of the 'triangular' trade, far outstripping Bristol in size and prosperity.

The simple reason why Liverpool was so successful in the slave trade was that the Liverpool shippers managed to sell slaves at £4 or £5 cheaper, a big saving when the average price of a slave in the West Indies was about £40. Liverpool had several advantages over Bristol. It was close to the centres where the goods for trade in West Africa were made, especially the cotton cloths of Lancashire and the hardware of Sheffield and Birmingham. Liverpool shippers kept their costs lower, partly by dodging customs duties (something they had got used to doing when trade was monopolized by London companies), and partly by their mean treatment of captains and crew. In the old days, when Bristol dominated trade and Liverpool was still a struggling little port, the captains, agents and factors of Bristol merchants were better paid, and had more privileges, than Liverpool skippers. In Bristol, a ship's captain dined ashore in style with a bottle of Madeira wine. In Liverpool, he had to eat salt beef in his cramped little cabin.

As Liverpool advanced, all this changed. By the middle of the century Liverpool was sending twice as many ships to West Africa as Bristol, and by the end of the century it had no rivals. By the time the trade was abolished, Liverpool had over sixty per cent of the entire British trade and over forty per cent of the entire European trade. One result was that Liverpool captains, in the slave trade at least, could demand better treatment. They had become the men on whom the fortunes of the town depended and were treated as local heroes, like the members of a cup-winning football team.

A slave-ship captain soon learned how to make money for himself by trading on the side, and he could rise to be a prosperous merchant himself. Bryan Blundell, a member of an old seafaring family who was born in 1675, commanded several

The Merchants

ships in the American trade and made a fortune of £7,500 by the time he retired from the sea. He became a ship-owner (and a slave-owner), and was involved in several different businesses. He is chiefly remembered today as the founder of a school for boys, just one of many proud old English institutions that owe their existence to the profits of the slave trade.

Although the triangular trade was a gamble – many ships were lost to enemy action or to the weather, and some merchants went bankrupt – it could be extremely profitable. The

Fashionable ladies liked to have Negro page-boys, whom they treated more as household pets than as children. This lady is the beautiful Louise de Kéroualle, Duchess of Portsmouth and Aubigny (1649–1734), favourite mistress of King Charles II of England.

average profit was about thirty per cent, an enormous amount in days when inflation hardly existed. As an annual sum, the profit worked out at about £300,000. Flowing into Liverpool each year, today that sum would be worth roughly £20,000,000.

The slave trade enriched everyone. For every big merchant who owned, in whole or in part, a dozen slave ships, there were hundreds of professional men, craftsmen and shopkeepers who had a small share in the trade. Shipbuilders, provision merchants, manufacturers of trade goods (and of iron fetters and thumbscrews), all lived off the Africans. Until the last twenty years or so of the eighteenth century very few people believed the trade was wrong. However, they never spoke of 'the slave trade', preferring to call it 'the African trade'; so perhaps they did have at the backs of their minds some qualms about selling human beings into slavery.

But in general Liverpool was proud of its enterprise and success. Before 1772, when slavery (but not the trade) was declared illegal in England, there were slaves to be seen in Liverpool itself as well as other British and European cities. Advertisements in the newspapers offered slaves for sale. Fashionable ladies were attended by black page-boys, and there are stories (though no firm evidence) of attractive young African women being privately traded as sex objects among the young gentlemen of Liverpool.

Ships Leaving Liverpool for Africa in the Eighteenth Century

Year	Number of Ships
1709	1
1730	15
1751	53
1761	69
1771	105
1781	43*
1791	102
1801	122

*War caused a depression in trade

The average number of slaves carried by a Liverpool ship in the late eighteenth century was about 330.

The Merchants

On the other side of the Atlantic, merchants of Massachusetts, Rhode Island and Connecticut also made fortunes from the slave trade, although most New England ship-owners were much smaller operators than their Liverpool counterparts. They had less money to spend, built smaller ships, and hired smaller crews. For a white sailor it was better to serve on an American slave ship, where discipline was less harsh and captains less tyrannical; but for the Africans it was probably worse, because conditions were cramped and the vessel often less seaworthy. Many New England ships were no larger, though older and in far worse shape, than a modern ocean-going yacht.

Slaving was only one part, though an important part, of the business of family firms like the prosperous Vernon brothers of Newport, Rhode Island. Newport, as one of its resident Christian ministers said, was 'built up by the blood of poor Africans'

Under the gorgeous dome of the Rotunda, New Orleans, a nineteenth-century estate is auctioned. Items for sale include pictures and slaves.

and in the second half of the eighteenth century it overtook Boston as the chief slave-trading centre.

They were sober citizens, these enterprising Yankees, who prided themselves on keeping up the strict morality of their Puritan ancestors and did not drink, swear or use bad language. But they were not above watering the rum which they sold to the Africans, or passing pewter off as silver. 'I'd plough the sea to porridge to make money,' proclaimed one of the rum-waterers, Simeon Potter of Bristol, Rhode Island. James de Wolf, member of a well-known slave-trading family, was charged with murder after he had ordered an African woman with smallpox to be thrown off one of his ships, but that did not prevent him being elected, years later, to the United States Senate.

Yankee merchants often became involved in the slave trade in a rather casual way. They exported New England products, like timber, and Newfoundland fish to the West Indies, where second-rate salted fish, not good enough for whites, became a large part of the diet of the slaves on the plantations. The main import from the West Indies, carried on the return voyage, was molasses; but sometimes slaves were carried too, and when the price of slaves in the West Indies went up, the New England ships found it worthwhile to trade direct in Guinea. As demand rose, and New England merchants entered big markets in the South such as Charleston, South Carolina (which also *exported* some slaves – American Indians – to the West Indies), the Guinea voyages became a regular thing. At times the Yankee skippers in West Africa discovered that so much New England rum had been traded there by their fellow-captains that they could not sell theirs and had to exchange it for manufactured goods from British ships.

The American War of Independence from Britain, which began in 1775, almost ended the American slave trade for a time. Newport was occupied by the British for three years, many owners lost all their ships, and the town never recovered its former position as the leading New England slave-trading port. At about this time it was declared illegal to import slaves into most of the middle and northern states, but, as the

The Merchants

House slaves in the American South were sometimes treated as members – subordinate members – of the family, and the babies of rich white parents knew their black nannies better than their own fathers and mothers. Although such slaves might be quite well treated, they had no rights in law against their owners, and could be sold away from their families like Uncle Tom in the famous novel, Uncle Tom's Cabin *(1852), by Harriet Beecher Stowe.*

The Savage Trade

demand for slaves existed mainly in the South, that decision had little effect in checking what a growing number of people had come to see as a beastly, cruel and immoral practice.

Instructions to a Slave Ship Captain

The following letter was sent to Captain Caesar Lawson by Thomas Leyland (see below) and Company, ship-owners and merchants of Liverpool, on 18 July 1803.

Sir,

Our ship *Enterprize*, to the command of which you are appointed, being now ready for sea, you are immediately to proceed to her, and make the best of your way to Bonny on the Coast of Africa. You will receive herewith an invoice of the Cargo on board her, which you are to barter at Bonny for prime Negroes, Ivory and Palm Oil. By law this vessel is allowed to carry 400 Negroes, and we request that they may be all males, if possible; at any rate, buy as few females as in your power, because we look to a Spanish market for the disposal of your cargo, where Females are a very tedious sale. In the choice of the Negroes be very particular, select those that are well-formed and strong; and do not buy any above 24 years of age, as it may happen that you will have to go to Jamaica, where you know any exceeding that age would be liable to a duty of £10 per head. While the slaves are on board the ship allow them every indulgence consistent with your own safety, and do not suffer any of your officers or crew to abuse or insult them in any respect ... A considerable part of our property under your care will not be insured, and we earnestly desire you to keep a particular look-out to avoid the enemy's cruisers, which are numerous, and you may hourly expect to be attacked by some of them. We request you will keep strict and regular discipline on board the ship; do not suffer drunkeness among any of your officers or crew, for it is sure to be attended with some misfortune, such as insurrection, mutiny and fire. Allow to the ship's company their regular portion of provisions, etc, and take every care of such as may get sick. You must keep the ship very clean and see that no part of her stores and materials are embezzled, neglected, or idly wasted. As soon as you have finished your trade and laid in a sufficient quantity of yams [a vegetable like sweet potato, staple diet of many Africans], wood, water and every other necessity for the Middle Passage, proceed with a press of sail for Barbadoes, and on your arrival there call

The Merchants

on Messrs Barton Higginson and Co., with whom you will find letters from us by which you are to be governed in prosecuting the remainder of the voyage ...

The *Enterprize* sailed two days later, and reached Bonny on 23 September. The price of a male African at Bonny at about this time was roughly £25, made up of eight different types of cloth, a large brass pan, two muskets, 25 kegs of powder, 100 flints (for muskets), two bags of shot, 20 knives, four iron pots, eight hats, four cutlasses, six bunches of beads, and 14 gallons of brandy.

The ship sailed from Bonny on 6 December, carrying 412 Africans (more than her legal limit), all Ibo. There were 194 men, 32 male youths, 66 boys, 42 women, 36 female youths and 42 girls. After calling for the letters at Barbados, the ship reached Havana, in Spanish Cuba, on 9 January. Despite the fears of the owners, all the slaves were sold except for one sick girl and nineteen people who died during the voyage. Leaving Havana on 28 March, the *Enterprize* arrived at Liverpool on 26 April. The following table shows the profits of the voyage:

Cost of fitting out ship and other expenses	£26,151
Cost of cargo (i.e. slaves)	£8,896
Total costs	£35,047
Sale of slaves	£41,475
Profit	£6,428

A Liverpool Merchant

Thomas Leyland, who had a fifty-per-cent share in the *Enterprize*, was a Yorkshireman. He came to Liverpool as a young man in 1770 and took a job as a clerk, but soon entered trade for himself in a modest way, with £500 borrowed from friends. He began to trade in Irish meat and bacon, and in 1776 he had a great stroke of luck when he won £20,000 in a state lottery. Having married his former employer's daughter – the size of his winnings made him a very desirable son-in-law – he

The Savage Trade

entered the slave trade in a big way. Within twenty years he had become one of the chief merchants in Liverpool and a partner in a bank. In 1806 he founded his own bank. A millionaire by this time, he served three times as Mayor of Liverpool. During his third term he gave one of the largest parties ever seen in Liverpool, in the Town Hall. Everyone of importance in Lancashire was present, from the Countess of Derby down to the officers of the local regiment. 'Everything,' said an eyewitness, 'that a lavish expenditure, combined with good taste, could do, was freely bestowed upon the entertainment; but what cannot be done in point of magnificence by a Mayor of Liverpool, who is also a banker and a millionaire... ?'

Thomas Leyland was only one of many vastly respected civic dignitaries in Britain whose status and fortune rested, in part at least, on the backs of the nations of Africa.

The tomb of an African servant boy, who died aged eighteen in 1720, near Bristol.

10

THE END OF THE TRADE

A WELL-KNOWN actor in the eighteenth century once appeared on the stage in Liverpool after drinking too much before the play began. The audience, observing his slurred speech and unsteady movements, began to jeer and hiss. The actor broke off his performance and marched down to the footlights. Planting his feet firmly on the boards he glared out at

Many people in the nineteenth century pointed out that the poor in Europe were no better off than slaves. In this cartoon of 1832, an anti-slavery speaker is holding forth on the benefits the English enjoy thanks to Magna Carta and the Reform Act (which had just been passed), while on the left is depicted the misery of a poor English family, labelled 'slavery', and on the right a happy family of American slaves, labelled 'freedom'. This was not an argument in favour of slavery; it was an argument against the system in Europe which condemned people to poverty and starvation.

The End of the Trade

the audience. As the noise died away, he declared in roaring tones that he had not come to be insulted by the people of a detestable town in which every brick was cemented with the blood of an African.

He spoke for a great many people. Early in the seventeenth century Richard Jobson had been disgusted by the idea of buying and selling people, and during the eighteenth century a growing number of people insisted that the trade was wrong, a blot on civilization which ought to be wiped away.

The Quakers were always opposed to the trade, even though some Quakers were slave-owners. They asked the question that no one could answer: if it was wrong to make slaves of whites, as almost everyone agreed, why was it not wrong to make slaves of blacks? Some Quakers refused to eat sugar made from cane because it was grown by slave labour. They made do with sugar from maple syrup.

Quaker influence in Pennsylvania, a colony founded by Quakers, lay behind the passing of a law by the colonial legislature which put a tax of £10 on every slave imported. So large a duty stopped the trade in Pennsylvania almost completely. Other colonies, including some in the South, also put restrictions on slave-trading, though the British government did not approve of their acts and slavery itself remained legal in all the thirteen colonies.

When the Americans broke away from Britain and declared their independence it looked as though slavery would be ended in the new republic. The Declaration of Independence (1776) stated that 'all men are created equal', and that surely meant that no man could be the slave of another. Thomas Paine, one of the prophets of the American Revolution, asked how any American colonist could claim the right to freedom from Britain if he were a slave-owner. Benjamin Franklin was an opponent of slavery, and although George Washington, the first President, owned slaves, John Adams, the second, refused to have any. Thomas Jefferson was a slave-owner, but a doubting one who freed his slaves in his will. Few of the other leaders who met to create the constitution of the new republic approved of slavery, still less the Atlantic slave trade; but the delegates from Georgia and South Carolina, the states most dependent on slaves, declared that they would not join the union if there were any attempt to interfere with slavery. The other delegates, deciding that the union of the thirteen states was more important than anything else, gave way to the Southerners, and slavery became an established institution in the United States of America. Wise men like Jefferson had grave misgivings, fearing that the future might have to pay a terrible price for the sins of the past. Time was to show their fears were real.

In Europe too opposition to the slave trade was rising. Granville Sharp, a civil servant in London, believed that slavery was illegal under the English constitution. He brought a case before the courts on behalf of a slave who had run away from his master, and after much legal argument the Lord Chief Justice laid down his famous judgment that no man could be a slave in England. It did not apply to the colonies, however, and it had no effect on the slave trade.

In 1785 another powerful enemy of the slave trade appeared on the scene when Thomas Clarkson won a prize at Cambridge University for an essay arguing that slavery was illegal. Clarkson was a rather silent, dogged young man who, if met at a party, probably seemed a bit of a bore. Soon after his prize-winning essay he had a religious vision of some kind which turned him into a fanatical opponent of the slave trade. As he had a small private income, Clarkson did not need to earn a living, and he devoted his whole life – and income – to the fight against slavery.

His activities made him very unpopular with those who depended on the slave trade for a living. Once, collecting facts about slave ships in Liverpool, he was walking back along a pier when he saw a group of nine seamen coming towards him. One of them he recognized as the murderer of a sailor; he had notes on the case. He retreated, but the men made straight for him. There was no one else about, and on either side of him a strong tide was running. A man pushed off the pier would never be seen again. But Clarkson was over six feet tall and heavily built. He surprised his opponents by suddenly drop-

The End of the Trade

Thomas Clarkson addressing a meeting of the Anti-Slavery Society, from a painting by Benjamin Haydon, 1840.

ping his shoulder and charging straight at them. He burst through to safety, leaving them swearing and staggering in his wake.

That frightening experience did not stop his investigation for a moment. Clarkson was a relentless seeker of facts. He had to make sure his evidence was reliable, and some of the stories he was told about the slave trade were so horrible that at first he doubted if they could be true and suspected that supporters of the trade were deliberately laying traps to ruin his reputation for honest reporting. He was ready to go to endless trouble to get his information. In London he heard of a sailor who could give him some information about slaving at Calabar. He did not know the man's name, nor where he lived, only that he was serving in a Royal Navy ship which was laid up in one of the dockyards. He at once set out to track the man down. Starting at nearby Deptford, he visited every laid-up warship to see if the man he wanted could be among the crew. Drawing a blank at Deptford, he tried Woolwich, then Chatham, then Sheerness, but with no better luck. Next he travelled to Portsmouth. The man was not there either, though the journey was not wasted as Clarkson discovered another sailor who gave him an eye-witness account of a brutal massacre by slave-dealers at Calabar in 1775. Still on the track of the nameless sailor he had first set out to find, the tireless Clarkson travelled farther west to Plymouth, where he visited in turn fifty-six warships. On the fifty-seventh he found his man. (He was, as it happens, Isaac Parker, whom we have already met at Calabar – see p. 49.) Altogether, Clarkson must have visited well over 300 ships, checking every member of the crew on each one.

Clarkson had some powerful supporters among the new class of industrialists, men like the great china manufacturer Josiah Wedgwood. With Clarkson and Granville Sharp, Wedgwood was one of the founders in 1787 of the Society for the Abolition of the Slave Trade.

In the same year, the cause of 'Abolition' gained its most valuable new member. William Wilberforce was a sincere Christian of that energetic sort who believe in clearing up slums before saying prayers. He was also a brilliant Member of Parliament and a close friend of William Pitt, the Prime Minister. Wilberforce became the leader of the Abolitionists in Parliament.

The opponents of Wilberforce called him a 'butterfly', but when the slave trade was discussed he proved to be a butterfly with teeth. Graceful, kindly and charming, Wilberforce seemed the natural opposite of the clumsy, dogged Clarkson, but both were determined men and together they made a strong team.

The End of the Trade

A china plaque by Wedgwood, copied from the seal of the Anti-Slavery Society, showing a chained African slave and the words, 'Am I not a man and a brother?' Thousands of copies of this plaque were made, and it was a powerful weapon of propaganda in the arsenal of the Abolitionists.

The Savage Trade

The End of the Trade

Clarkson did the hard work of research, digging out the facts which then became the basis for Wilberforce's attacks on the slave trade in Parliament.

In France also opposition to the slave trade was rising, led by a society called Les Amis des Noirs ('the Friends of the Blacks'). When the French Revolution broke out in 1789, Clarkson travelled to Paris hoping to get the co-operation of the new National Assembly against the slave trade. But many people in France were suspicious of the Englishman, even accusing him of being a spy, and a reaction against the Abolitionists' cause set in after a bloody rebellion of the slaves in the French colony of Haiti. The prospect of a slave revolt frightened all Europeans who had interests in the plantation colonies. In London, Samuel Johnson used to annoy many of his acquaintances by raising his glass and proposing a toast to 'the success of the next slave revolt in Jamaica'.

The speeches of Wilberforce and the horror stories unearthed by Clarkson brought the slave trade into the public eye. People who had never given much thought to the subject read the speeches and reports of the Abolitionists and were shocked by what they read. Indignation against the trade began to rise, and it was helped by the often ridiculous arguments of those who supported the trade. When sailors were flogged on a slave ship, said the Liverpool ship-owners, it was always done out of hearing of the slaves, so they should not be upset. No one who was not simple-minded believed that. The reason why Africans were so distressed when they were parted from their families, the public was told, was that Africans are highly sexed and feared that they would get no sex in slavery. Reasonable people could hardly swallow such gross and inhuman explanations. Wilberforce and his friends made mincemeat of them.

For twenty years Wilberforce spoke out against the slave trade and introduced motions in Parliament calling for an end to it. They were defeated in the vote, but the majority against

A wax effigy of William Wilberforce sitting in the study of his house in Hull, which is now a museum of the anti-slavery movement.

Former slaves in the United States celebrating President Lincoln's Proclamation, copies of which are being joyfully waved about, which gave them their freedom.

grew smaller every year, and it became obvious that the success of Abolition was only a matter of time.

It was not the propaganda of the Abolitionists alone that spelled the doom of the slave trade. The trade was no longer a vital part of the British economy. Throughout most of the eighteenth century the West Indian sugar-growers and the merchants connected with them had a powerful voice in government policy because the national economy depended on them. By the end of the century that was no longer true. Britain was becoming an industrial state, growing rich from the sale of its manufactures, and the new industrialists, Wedgwood and his kind, were replacing the old land-owners and merchants of what was called 'the West India interest'. Britain's prosperity rested less and less on the sugar colonies, more and more on the factories of Manchester and Birmingham. The slave trade, in one word, was no longer 'necessary'.

In 1806 a new government came to power with George Fox

The End of the Trade

as Prime Minister. He was an old opponent of the slave trade, and though he was to die within a few months, he succeeded in having a government motion for abolition passed by both Houses of Parliament – and by a surprisingly large majority. In 1807 the slave trade became illegal for British subjects.

Britain was not the first country to abolish the slave trade. That honour belonged to Denmark, in 1802. But Britain was by far the largest slave-trading nation and, having given up the trade themselves, the British were anxious to prevent others making a profit out of it. British cruisers in African waters tried to prevent the smuggling of slaves, and British diplomats urged other countries to follow Britain's example. Sweden abolished the trade in 1813, the Netherlands in 1814, Portugal and Spain soon afterwards, and France in 1818, though at first the French made no serious effort to enforce the new law.

Granville Sharp rescuing a slave from his master. This incident (painted a century later by James Hayllar) led to a lawsuit in 1767 which resulted in the judgment that no man can be a slave on English soil.

CAUTION!!
COLORED PEOPLE
OF BOSTON, ONE & ALL,

You are hereby respectfully CAUTIONED and advised, to avoid conversing with the

Watchmen and Police Officers of Boston,

For since the recent ORDER OF THE MAYOR & ALDERMEN, they are empowered to act as

KIDNAPPERS
AND
Slave Catchers,

And they have already been actually employed in KIDNAPPING, CATCHING, AND KEEPING SLAVES. Therefore, if you value your LIBERTY, and the *Welfare of the Fugitives* among you, *Shun* them in every possible manner, as so many *HOUNDS* on the track of the most unfortunate of your race.

Keep a Sharp Look Out for KIDNAPPERS, and have TOP EYE open.

APRIL 24, 1851.

The End of the Trade

As long as slavery itself existed, the slave trade – legally or not – went on. Although the importing of slaves was forbidden in most American states, it continued just the same. Between 1804 and 1807 no less than 200 slave ships arrived at Charleston, South Carolina. A few British cruisers, which in any case could not interfere with ships flying an American or French flag, could do very little. 'Trying to stop the slave trade with cruisers', said one British naval officer, 'is like trying to stop a river by building a dam across its mouth.'

Those who had led the fight against the slave trade in England turned their hostility against slavery itself. Wilberforce died in 1833, a few weeks before the passing of an Act of Parliament which declared slavery illegal in the British Empire. African rulers were persuaded to sign treaties that banned the slave trade in their territories, though most of them soon forgot those inconvenient bits of paper. A law in the United States which was supposed to end slave-trading altogether was generally ignored. In 1844 a British official in Sierra Leone reported to the Foreign Secretary 'that the slave trade is increasing, and that it is conducted perhaps more systematically than it has ever been hitherto'.

In the United States slavery was not ended until North and South had fought a bitter civil war and President Abraham Lincoln had issued his famous Proclamation of Emancipation in 1862. Less than ten years later slavery came to an end in Brazil, the last great slave-owning society in the New World, and with that the Atlantic slave trade at last ceased, over four hundred years after it had begun. Slave-trading still continued in East Africa, where it was controlled mainly by Arabs, but

Before the American Civil War, slaves who escaped from their owners in the South found sanctuary in the North, in places like Boston, where feelings against slavery ran high. This poster warns the people of Boston to beware of 'slave catchers' who were employed to recapture the runaways. In the famous Dred Scott case of 1857, the Supreme Court ruled that a slave, or the descendant of a slave, could not be a U.S. citizen and that Congress had no power to forbid slavery in any part of the United States. This decision enraged the opponents of slavery and helped to provoke the events which led to civil war.

The Savage Trade

The Atlantic slave trade ended, but slavery continued elsewhere. This picture shows African slaves being freed by a British expedition in 1874.

The slave market in Zanzibar, chief centre of the slave trade in East Africa, in 1872. It was closed down a year later and a cathedral built on the site.

The End of the Trade

the closing of the ancient slave market in Zanzibar in 1872 heralded the end of the trade there also. Slavery did not disappear completely, and perhaps has not vanished yet, but the horrors of the slave auction, and of the foul-smelling ships that for four centuries carried over twenty million people into slavery across the Atlantic, were gone for ever. They left behind a legacy of hate and distrust that is not dead yet.

The society of ancient Rome was founded on slavery, and the conquests of the Roman armies ensured a large supply of captives to be enslaved. The Roman lady in her litter, in this imaginative reconstruction of a Roman street in the time of Augustus (27 B.C.–A.D. 14), is attended by Nubian slaves from Africa.

Slavery in History

Slavery was nothing new. As far back as history recorded, human societies all over the world had been slave-owners more often than not. In ancient Greece slavery was defended by the philosophers. Even those who disliked it believed it was necessary. Without slaves, they realized, there would be no philosophy, as philosophers would be too busy sowing and ploughing to sit down and think. Two thousand years after Aristotle decided that slavery was necessary, the French philosopher Voltaire agreed that it was inevitable. Slavery, he said, is as ancient as human nature itself.

This painting by M. H. Shaw illustrates a famous incident (perhaps true perhaps not) in Rome in the time of Pope Gregory I (590–604), the greatest of the early Popes. In the slave market one day he saw some pretty, fair-haired boys for sale. He was told they were Angli, *'Angles', or English, and replied,* 'Non Angli sed angeli', *'Not Angles but angels.' Later, he sent St Augustine to convert the English to Christianity.*

The Savage Trade

Strange as it seems, slavery could be a benefit. Non-slaves could be oppressed and exploited worse than slaves, who, because they were someone's property, were treated with more care. But for other people, slavery could be the worst fate imaginable. Of course there is no single condition of 'slavery'. The word is misleading because it can stand for different things. In some Eastern countries it was possible for a man who was technically a slave to become richer and more powerful than those who were not. The greatest of the sultans of Delhi in the thirteenth century began his career as a palace slave.

The Romans were slave-owners like the Greeks. The masters in ancient Rome had total authority over their slaves, who could not own property nor be legally married, and could be put to death at their master's order. Yet the oppression of Roman slaves was only a little more severe than the oppression of Roman wives and children, and as time passed the conditions of slavery became easier. Slaves could be freed by their masters. It was even possible for them to become officials of government. Some of the greatest men of the Roman Empire were former slaves.

The huge numbers of Roman slaves – they far outnumbered free citizens – were mostly captives taken in Rome's wars. Julius Caesar once sold over 60,000 prisoners as slaves after a battle against the Gauls. Slaves were needed, above all, to work in the fields, where they lived in grim barracks and led a cruelly hard life. The fortunate ones became household slaves, a much more comfortable position as a rule. Slaves were also used for other tasks by the Romans, and this included providing the bloodthirsty form of entertainment in which trained fighting slaves called gladiators fought to the death in a public arena.

Slavery in History

Serfs under an overseer harvesting wheat, from a fourteenth-century English manuscript. Serfs in medieval Europe did have some rights, but in many ways they were little better than slaves.

In the later years of the Roman Empire the division between slaves and others almost disappeared, and in medieval Europe slavery was uncommon, though the condition of serfdom, in which most peasants lived, may not have seemed much different. A serf was bound to the land: he was part of the amenities, like hunting rights or a stand of timber. He had to work for his master, or lord, without payment, but he could not be sold, like a slave, and the duties he owed his lord were balanced by obligations which his lord had towards him. Serfs were the native people of a country, often a conquered people like the Anglo-Saxon English under Norman rule. They were not prisoners of war, as slaves most often were.

Serfdom lasted a long while. In Russia it was not legally abolished until the nineteenth century and, in some obscure parts of the world where newspaper reporters and TV cameras are seldom seen, serfdom and other forms of near-slavery still exist.

Roman citizens, instead of going to a football match, went to watch grimmer 'sports', like the fights between gladiators in the Colosseum. The victorious gladiator looks up to the spectators, whose thumbs-down signal means he should kill his vanquished opponent. Thumbs-up would have meant, 'Let him live.' (Actually, no one now is quite certain that 'thumbs-down' meant 'death' and 'thumbs-up' meant 'life'; it may have been the other way about.)

The Savage Trade

In Africa, too, slavery has a long history. It was not always a story of Europeans enslaving Africans. In the period when the European slave trade in West Africa was beginning, thousands of Europeans who had been captured in war, kidnapped, or sold by their own people, worked as slaves for the Muslim inhabitants of North Africa. The city of Tunis alone, it was said, contained 30,000 Christian slaves. Slaves in hundreds were forced to row the many-oared warships of the Mediterranean. After the great sea battle of Lepanto in 1571, when the Ottoman Turks and their allies were defeated by an allied Christian fleet, 15,000 Christian slaves were released from the chains that bound them to their benches in the Turkish galleys.

Slavery in History

At the battle of Lepanto (1571) in the Mediterranean, a Christian force made up of ships from Venice, Spain, Genoa and the Papal States defeated the fleet of the Muslim Turks. The Turkish ships were galleys, oared vessels rowed by Christian slaves who had been captured in earlier battles. Naturally, the Christian galley slaves wanted their masters to lose, and that may have been a factor in the result of the battle.

The Savage Trade

Slavery in Africa south of the Sahara Desert was not introduced by Europeans. It existed there from the earliest times. When the Scottish explorer Mungo Park returned from his expedition to the Niger River in 1796, he reckoned that about three quarters of the people he had seen during his journey through a part of Africa unknown to Europeans had been slaves. Many of those transported across the Atlantic in the European slave ships had been slaves in their own country. Clara, a slave in Jamaica in the eighteenth century, told her owner she had once been a slave in the Gold Coast (modern Ghana). When her African master died, she had been sold to European slavers to pay his debts, and by them transported to Jamaica.

Europeans who defended the slave trade made the most of the fact that slavery existed inside Africa also; but in reality African slavery was nothing like what Europeans had understood by the word since the days of the Romans. African slavery was much more like European serfdom. In Africa slaves had certain rights and owners had certain duties – to feed, clothe, shelter and protect their slaves. Slaves were often treated kindly, more like members of the family than creatures of an inferior species. In some countries slaves could not be sold except in special circumstances. In other parts, a slave might marry the daughter of the king or even become a king himself. Slaves were allowed to earn money, and were sometimes able to buy their freedom. European visitors to West Africa reported cases of slaves who through their own skill in trade had become richer than their masters and owned slaves of

their own. None of these things was possible for a slave on a West Indian sugar plantation.

How did people become slaves in Africa? One way was to be captured in a war, and this became the most common method of getting slaves in the days of the European trade. Slaves taken in war were usually not so well treated; they were less likely to become household slaves and members of the family. Slavery was enforced as a punishment for theft and other crimes in many parts of Africa, and it sometimes happened that a man who was in debt might sell himself – or his whole family – into slavery to work off the debt. Slaves of that kind were more likely to be able to regain their freedom one day. Although slaves *were* bought and sold, slave-trading was never the huge profit-making enterprise that Europeans made it. There was brutality in African slavery too, but slaves were not treated as an inferior kind of people doomed to eternal subjection. They only experienced that kind of slavery if they had the ill luck to be sold to Europeans.

Serfdom continued on Russian estates long after it had ended in other European countries, and under a severe master the life of a Russian serf was grim indeed. Tsar Alexander II (1855–81) remarked, 'It is better to abolish serfdom from above than to wait until it begins to be abolished from below,' and in 1861 the Russian peasants became free. However, freeing the peasants from serfdom did not, as Alexander hoped, end the danger of revolution, although it was not until 1917 that the 'old régime' in Russia of tsars and aristocratic landowners was overthrown.

Illustrations and Acknowledgements

Frontispiece Zanzibar slave boy. United Society for the Propagation of the Gospel.

p. 6   Prince Henry of Portugal. Detail from a painting by Nuno Gonçalves. Mansell Collection.

p. 9   Portuguese caravel. National Maritime Museum.

p. 13   Map of Africa. From the Catalan Atlas, made about 1375 and presented to The King of France. Bibliothèque Nationale, Paris.

p. 15   Columbus landing on Watling Island. From *Americae Partes*, 1590. Radio Times Hulton Picture Library.

p. 16   Arawak Indians. Smithsonian Institution Bureau of Ethnology 25th Annual Report.

p. 17   Bartolomé de las Casas. Radio Times Hulton Picture Library.

p. 19   John Hawkins. Painting by Custodis, 1591. Buckland Abbey, Devon.

p. 19   Hawkins's flagship, *Jesus of Lubeck*. Miniature painting from a manuscript. By permission of the Master and Fellows of Magdalene College, Cambridge.

p. 27   Bronze figure of a sixteenth-century Portuguese soldier. Photo: Werner Forman Archive.

p. 27   African craftsmen working iron. British Museum.

p. 28   African town. From Francis Moore, *Travels into the Inland Parts of Africa*, 1738. Senate House Library, University of London.

p. 29   Cowrie shells. Photo: Heather Angel.

p. 31   Coronation of the King of Whydah, French West Africa, 1725. Engraved by G. Child. Radio Times Hulton Picture Library.

p. 33   Seventeenth-century drawing of a hippopotamus. Radio Times Hulton Picture Library.

p. 33   Seventeenth-century drawing of a giraffe. Radio Times Hulton Picture Library.

p. 35   Rosehall, a plantation house in Jamaica. Anne Bolt.

p. 36   Slaves on a West Indian sugar plantation. Mary Evans Picture Library.

p. 38   Sugar barrels being unloaded at Bristol, *c*. 1800. Radio Times Hulton Picture Library.

Illustrations and Acknowledgements

p. 39 Slaves planting sugar cane on a West Indian plantation. From Robert Bridgen, *West India Sketches*. Royal Commonwealth Society.

p. 40 Interior of a boiling house. Royal Commonwealth Society.

p. 41 Punishing a slave in Brazil. Radio Times Hulton Picture Library.

p. 42 Rain forest river scene in West Africa. Radio Times Hulton Picture Library.

p. 45 Africans at a British post in West Africa trying out guns. From J. Dupuis, *Journal of a Residence in Ashanti*, 1824. Hamlyn Group.

pp. 48–9 The British fort at Winneba, 1727. Royal Commonwealth Society.

p. 50 Slave raiders attacking a village. From a print published in 1809. Cornell University Library.

p. 51 Slave chaingang in Africa, c. 1894. Radio Times Hulton Picture Library.

p. 54 Inspection and sale of a slave. Library of Congress.

p. 56 Village scene in Ashanti (Ghana). Mary Evans Picture Library.

p. 62 Title page of Olaudah Equiano's autobiography. Senate House Library, University of London.

p. 65 Slave revolt on board ship. H. Roger Viollet.

p. 69 Modern photograph of El Mina, West Africa. Aerofilms.

p. 69 Eighteenth-century view of Cape Coast Castle. Royal Commonwealth Society.

p. 73 Nicholas Owen's house on the River Sherbro. From N. Owen, *Journal of a Slave Dealer.* Senate House Library, University of London.

p. 76 Drawing of 'Dancing Priests' made by Nicholas Owen. From *Journal of a Slave Dealer*. Senate House Library, University of London.

p. 79 Map of the routes of the slave-trade during the eighteenth century.

p. 81 The Rev. John Newton. By J. Russell. National Portrait Gallery.

p. 84 Slaves on the way to the West Indies forced to dance on the ship's deck. Early nineteenth century. Mary Evans Picture Library.

p. 84 Handcuffs and thumbscrews for use on slaves. From Thomas Clarkson, *History of the Abolition of the Slave Trade*, 1808. Senate House Library, University of London.

p. 85 Branding iron. Wilberforce House Museum, Hull.

p. 86 Below decks on a slave ship. National Maritime Museum.

p. 88 The Africans of the slave bark *Wildfire. Harpers Weekly*, 1860.

p. 89 Poster advertising the sale of slaves. U.S.A., early nineteenth century. Wilberforce House Museum, Hull.

The Savage Trade

p. 92 Plan for stowing slaves on the *Brookes* of Liverpool. From Clarkson's *Abstract of the Evidence*, 1791. Wilberforce House Museum, Hull.

p. 95 Slaves thrown overboard. Radio Times Hulton Picture Library.

p. 97 Captain Hugh Crow. From his *Memoirs*, 1830. Bodleian Library, Oxford.

pp. 100–101 Action between the *Mary*, Crow's ship, and two English warships. From H. Crow, *Memoirs*, 1830. Bodleian Library, Oxford.

p. 103 Queen Square, Bristol. Photo: Reece Winstone.

p. 104 Old Exchange, Liverpool. Guildhall Library.

pp. 104–5 Liverpool, south-east prospect, *c.* 1770. Liverpool Records Office.

p. 107 The Duchess of Portsmouth. Painting by Pierre Mignard. Radio Times Hulton Picture Library.

p. 109 Auction under the Rotunda, New Orleans. The Bettmann Archive, Inc.

p. 111 Slave life on a Deep South Plantation. Peter Newmark's Western Americana.

p. 114 Tomb of an African servant boy. Henbury, Bristol. Photo: Reece Winstone.

p. 116 Cartoon from the *Looking Glass*, 1832. Manchester Public Libraries.

p. 119 Thomas Clarkson addressing a meeting of the Anti-Slavery Society. From a painting by Benjamin Haydon, 1840. National Portrait Gallery.

p. 121 China plaque by Wedgwood, copied from the seal of the Anti-Slavery Society. Wedgwood.

p. 122 Wax effigy of William Wilberforce. Wilberforce House Museum, Hull.

p. 124 Former slaves celebrating the decrees of enfranchisement proclaimed by President Lincoln. Radio Times Hulton Picture Library.

p. 125 Granville Sharp rescuing a slave from his master. From a painting by James Hayllar, 1864. Wilberforce House Museum, Hull.

p. 126 Poster telling runaway slaves to beware of slave catchers. Peter Newark's Western Americana.

p. 128 African slaves being freed by a British expedition in 1874. Mansell Collection.

p. 128 The Slave Market in Zanzibar, 1872. Mansell Collection.

p. 130 'The Appian Way in the time of Augustus' by Boulanger. Victorian mezzotint. Mansell Collection.

p. 131 'Not Angles but Angels' by M. H. Shaw. Victorian mezzotint. Mansell Collection.

Illustrations and Acknowledgements

p. 132 'Pollice Verso' by Gerome, *c.* 1870. Radio Times Hulton Picture Library.

p. 133 A fourteenth-century overseer. From a manuscript in the British Museum. Radio Times Hulton Picture Library.

pp. 134–5 The Battle of Lepanto, 1571. Sixteenth century, artist unknown. National Maritime Museum.

p. 136 Landowner and serfs in Russia, 1789. From an engraving by Fittler. Mansell Collection.

Index

Numbers in italics indicate illustrations

Abolition: campaign for, 96, 117–20, *121*, 122–7; of slavery, 108, 127, 129; of slave trade, 96, 102, *124*, 124–5, 127, *128*
Adams, John, 117
Africa, *13*; European attitudes to, 30–1, 34; independent states of, 43–4; slavery in, 134, 136–7; *see also* North Africa, West Africa
Africans: craftsmen, 26, *27*; rulers, *13*, 30–1, *31*, 45–6, 58–9, 73, 127; slaves, *frontispiece*, 26, *51*, 58, 63; slave-traders, 44–7, 49–54, 60–61; *see also* West Africans
Alexander II, Tsar, 137
America: Abolition of slavery in, *124*, 127; attitudes to slavery in, *41*, *111*, *116*, 117–18, *126*; slave imports, 110; 117, 127; slave-ships, 78, 109; slave trade, 78–9, *109*, 109–10, 112; War of Independence, 110
American Indians, 26, 110
Amis des Noirs, Les, 123
Angola, 80, 103
Ann, 92–4
Ansa, Kwame, 68
Anti-Slavery Society, 120, *121*
Arabs, 7, 127
Arawak Indians, *16*
Aristotle, 131
Atkins, John, 63, 66
Auguina, Queen of, 47–9
Azurara, Gomes Eannes de, 10–12

Baillie (or Brainie), William, 52–5
Barbados, 37, 113
Barbot, Jean, 46, 71–2
Benin, 30
Blundell, Bryan, 106–7
Bojador, Cape, 7, 8
Brainie, *see* Baillie
Brazil, 127, *41*
Bristol, *38*, *103*, 105, 106, *114*
Britain: interests in Guinea, 43; slavery in, 108, 118; slave trade, 105, 125, 127, 128; *see also* Bristol, England, Liverpool
British slave-traders, 72–7, 80, 82, 84, 97–9, 102, 105–8, 113, 115
Brookes, 92, 87, 91

Cabess (or Kabes), John, 52–5
Caboceers, 46–7, 52–4
Calabar, 47, 49, 52, 120
Cape Coast Castle, 47, 67, 68, *69*, 70–71
Caribbean, *see* West Indies
Ceuta, 14
Christians, 11, 47, 103, 110, 120, 134
Clarkson, Thomas, 87, 118–19, *119*, 120, 123
Collingwood, Captain Luke, 94
Columbus, Christopher, 15, *15*
Commenda, Fort, 52–3, 70–71
Conga, 20–21
Crow, Captain Hugh, 83, 87, 90, *97*, 97–9, 102

Denmark, 125
Diseases, tropical, 43, 71, 77
Drake, Richard, 83, 85
Dutch traders, 48–9, 67, 70, 71
Dysentery, 87

Eannes, Gil, 7, 8
Ebro, Dick, 49–50
El Mina, castle of, 67, 68, *69*, 70
England: attitudes to slavery in, 23, 117, 118–20, 123–4, *125*; *see also* Britain
English traders, 18, *19*, 20–3, 24, 44, 47–9, 52–4, 64, 70
Enterprize, 112–13
Equiano, Olaudah, *56*, 57–62, *62*, 65, 66
Europe, 37; poverty in, *116*
Europeans: in Africa, 67–8, 70–72; African attitudes to, 70; attitudes to Africans, 30–31, 34, 42, 43, 46, 75, 103; as slaves, 134; *see also* Ships, in slave trade; Slave-traders; Traders

142

Index

Falconbridge, Alexander, 85–6, 87
Forts, European, *49*, 67–8, *69*, 70–72
Fox, George, 125
France: colonies, 40–41; opposition to slave trade in, 123, 125; privateers, 20; traders, 18, 46, 70, 71–2

Gambia, 23, 42, 44
Ghana, 26, *56: see also* Gold Coast
Gold, 8, 14–16, 24, 43, 46
Gold Coast, 46, 47–9, *49*, 52, 68, 71, 80, 136
Grandy King George, 47
Greece, slavery in, 131
Guinea, 29, 43–4, 47, 68, 78, 79–80, 91, 103
Guns, trade in, 44, *45*

Haiti, slave rebellion in, 123
Hawkins, John, 18, *19*, 20–23, 24, 44
Henry, Prince, 'the Navigator', *6*, 7, 8, 10–11

Ibo, 57–9, 113
Industrial Revolution, 37
Insurance of slaves at sea, 95–6, 98

Jamaica, 34, *35*, 112, 123, 136
Jefferson, Thomas, 117
Jesus of Lubeck, 18, *19*
Jobson, Richard, 23–4, 25, 117
Johnson, Samuel, 123
Julius Caesar, 132

Kabes, *see* Cabess
Kidnapping raids, 44, 45, 49–50, *50*, *51*, 51–2, 60–61, *126–7*
King David, 93
Kongo, kingdom of, 31
Krumen, 80

Lançarote's expedition, 8–9, 11, 15
Las Casas, Bartolomé de, *17*, 17–18
Lepanto, Battle of, 134, *134–5*
Leyland, Thomas, 112, 113, 115
Lincoln, Abraham, 127
Liverpool, *104–5*, 105–6; merchants, 80, 106–7 112–15; ships, 91, 97–9, 102, 108
Livingstone, David, 32, 34

McTaggart, Captain, 83
Malagueta pepper, 15
Malaria, 43, 77
Mansa, Musa, *13*
Mansfield, Lord, 96
Mary, 99, *100–101*
Merchants, *see* Traders

Miles, William, 37–8
Moore, Francis, 28, 44
Muslims, 14, 134

Netherlands, 125; *see also* Dutch traders
New Orleans, auction in, *109*
Newport, Rhode Island, 109–10
Newton, Rev. John, *81*, 82–3
Niger River, 42, 57, 136
North Africa, *13*, 13–14, 134

Old Calabar, 47, 49, 52, 120
Ottoman Turks, Christian slaves of, 134, *134–5*
Ouidah, *see* Whydah
Owen, Blayney, 73–4, 75
Owen, Nicholas, 72–7, *73*

Paine, Thomas, 117
Park, Mungo, 136
Parker, Isaac, 49–52, 120
Pepple, King, 98
Portugal, 10–11, 15, 125
Portuguese, 7, 14, *27*, 68; in Africa, 14–15, 30–31, 67, 68, 70; slave-traders, *6*, 8, *9*, 10–11, 14–15, 18, 20, 103
Prisoners-of-war as slaves, 20–21, 44, 45, 132, 136–7
Profits, from slave trade, 108, 113

Quakers, 66, 117

Revolts, 64–5, *65*, 91, 93, 123
Roberts, Captain, Bartholomew, 63
Rome, ancient, slavery in, *130, 131, 132*, 132–3
Royal African Company, 44, 52, 67–8, 70, 105
Rum boats, 78, 110
Russia, serfdom in, 133, *136–7*

Sahel empires, 26
Sailors on slave-ships, 83, 87, 91, 93, 98, 123
Sale of slaves, *54, 89*, 90, 106, 108, *109*, 113, *128*
San Juan de Ullua, 23
Sano, Bucknor, 23, 24
Scurvy, 85
Senegal, 42
Serfdom, 133, *133, 136–7*
Sharp, Granville, 96, 118, 120
Sherbro River, 72, 74, 77
Ships, in slave trade, 78–102, 108, 129; American, 78, 109; battles at sea, 89, 99, *100–101*; captains of,

Ships—*cont.*
88, 106; conditions on, *92*, 83–4, *84–6*, 85–90, *88*, 94, 112; European, *9, 13*, 18, *19*, 78, 80, 91, 93–4, 97–9, 102, 108, 112–13; murder of slaves on, 94–5, *95*, 96, 110; routes, map of, *79*; slave revolts on, 64–5, *65*, 91, 93–4

Sierra Leone, 72, 127

Slave-raiders, 49–50, *50, 51*, 51–2

Slavery: in history, 131–4, *131–6*, 136–7; justification of; 11, 123; opposition to, 96, 117–20, *121*, 122–7, *128*; as punishment for crime, 137; *see also* Abolition

Slaves: death rate at sea, 87; European, 134; massacres of, 94–5, *95*, 96, 110, 120; melancholy among, 87; revolts by, 63–5, *65*, 91, 93–4, 123; sale of, *54, 89*, 90, 91, 106, 108, *109*, 113, *128*; smuggling of, 125, 127; *see also* America, Ships, West Indies, *and individual countries*

Slave-traders, 54, 63, 72–7, 103–15; African, 44–7, 49–54, 60–61; American, 109–10, 112; British, 72–7, 80, 81, 83, 97–9, 102, 105–8, 113, 115; Dutch, 103; English, 18, *19*, 20–3, 24, 44; Portuguese, 8–11, 14–15, 18, 20, 103; *see also* Ships

Spain, 125

Spanish colonies, *16*; English slave trade with, 21–3; slavery in, 17–18

Sugar, West Indian, *38*; plantations, *35, 36, 39*; production, 35, *36*, 37–8, *39, 40*, 40, 124

Sweden, 125

Tomba, Captain, 63–4

Trade, 14–15, 23–4, 70, 110; cheating in, 46–7, 52–3, 72, 110; forts, 67–8, *69*, 70–72; post, *45*; triangular, 78, 106, 107; West African, 15, 29–30, 44, 59, 76; West Indian, 15, 29–30, 37–8, 44, 110

Traders, 103–15; European, 18, 23, 46–9, 52–4, 68, 70–77; independent, 67, 77; West African, 46; *see also* Slave-traders

Trotter, Dr Thomas, 87, 91

Tsetse flies, 43

Tunis, 134

USA, *see* America

Verde, Cape, 20

Voltaire, 131

Washington, George, 117

Wedgwood, Josiah, 120

West Africa: slavery in, 58, 136; slave trade, 44–5, 49–54, 59–65, 72–3, 77, 78; society in, 29–30, 32, 34, 59; spiritual life, 32, 59; trade, 15, 29–30, 44, *45*, 59, 76; trade forts, *49*, 67–8, *69*, 70–72

West Africans: European attitudes to, 30–31, 34, 42, 43, 46, 75; slaves, 26; traders, 46

West Indies, 15–18, 124; plantations, 34, *35, 36, 39*; slaves in, 17–18, 26, 35, *36, 39*, 40, 106, 112; sugar production, 35, *36*, 37–8, *39, 40*, 40, 124; trade, 15, 29–30, 37–8, 44, 110

Whydah, 70, *31*

Wilberforce, William, 120, *122*, 123, 127

Wildfire, 88

Winneba, 47–8, *49*

Wolf, James de, 110

Zanzibar, *frontispiece, 128*, 129

Zong, 94–5, *95*, 96